Windows

Enterprise Desktop

Support Technician

(EDST7)

70-685

Study Guide

Alan Frasier

Sean Odom

MediaWorks Publishing

Enterprise Desktop Support Technician (EDST7) 70-685 Study Guide

ISBN: 145057436X

EAN-13: 9781450574365

Alan's Acknowledgements

I'd like to thank my wonderful wife Tirshawna, for being the best part of my day, and lovingly accepting my faults. My mother and father Alan and Linda who are always there for me. My two sisters Tiffanie and Julie, my friend and colleague Jonathan Martinez, and my favorite family north of Medford, South of Seattle, the Morales'.

Sean's Acknowledgements

I have to thank many of those who care about me the most. The ones that have said lately, "Even when I am home. I am not home." Also to the person who gives me a day job and has too much faith in me, Randy Bankofier. I must also include the people that support me at work. They include Mark Eames, Risa Fitzsimmons, and Alan Frazier for helping finish this book.

Also I have to acknowledge a few really great friends and customers. Marc Tamarin at Virtual IT Consulting, Dr. Chestler at Gateway Eye Clinic, Seth and Rick Edvalson with IntegriNet, Matt at Pacific Trading Inland, Reymond at Montgomery and Graham, Sam Wheat at the Microsoft Corporation, Todd Lammle at Globalnet Solution, and many others including all of my students over the years.

Also, I need to thank the entire team that worked together to write, edit, and get this book on the shelves in the limited amount of time we had to do it.

Table of Contents

Introduction

This study guide book should be used to help you understand the subjects and materials you need to pass the Microsoft certification exam 70-685. This book should be used as only a tool in preparing for the test and to review your knowledge of the subject matter. This book is not intended to teach you everything you need to know about a given topic.

The author has investigated the exam topics and questions and provided content based on the questions and problems that you're likely to encounter on a test. The MediaWorks Publishing, Exam Study Guide Series books work to bring together as much information as possible about each Microsoft certification exam they intend to educate you on.

The MCTS (Microsoft Certified Technology Specialist) for *Windows 7, Configure* (70-680) exam certification is the foundation of the Windows 7 certification series. This exam requires you to have a strong knowledge of the operating systems features, feature requirements, how to install the operating system, configuring exam covered options, and how to troubleshoot the Windows 7 operating system installation. You should have a good understanding of the legacy features of the operating system as well as the new features of the operating system when you finish this book as well.

The MCITP (Microsoft Certified IT Professional) for the *Enterprise Desktop Support Technician 7(EDST7)* is the next step in the certification process for Windows 7. This new certification is the most unique of any previous Microsoft certification. It actually requires a third party exam to complete this certification. Microsoft has never really taken a focus on customer service in any certification path until now.

The screenshot in figure I.1 shows the certification path information from the Help Desk Institute's website. HDI teamed up with Microsoft to provide the exam and as well as training opportunities to complete this new certification by offering two different exams.

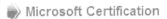 Microsoft Certification

Microsoft | Learning

C E R T I F I E D

The *Microsoft MCITP: Enterprise Desktop Support Technician 7 Credential* will require one of two HDI certifications: HDI Support Center Analyst (HDI-SCA) or HDI Desktop Support Technician (HDI-DST).

This certification will validate that Microsoft Certified IT Professionals who specialize in Desktop Support for Windows 7 understand both the technical aspects of the operating system as well as the vital customer service and business process skills required by support professionals.

Certification Path | Prepare For Your Exam | Purchase Your Exam

Choose
Your
Certification
Path

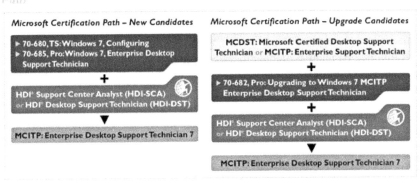

Microsoft Certification Path – New Candidates

▸ 70-680, TS: Windows 7, Configuring
▸ 70-685, Pro: Windows 7, Enterprise Desktop Support Technician

+

HDI° Support Center Analyst (HDI-SCA)
or HDI° Desktop Support Technician (HDI-DST)

▼

MCITP: Enterprise Desktop Support Technician 7

Microsoft Certification Path – Upgrade Candidates

MCDST: Microsoft Certified Desktop Support Technician or MCITP: Enterprise Support Technician

+

▸ 70-682, Pro: Upgrading to Windows 7 MCITP Enterprise Desktop Support Technician

+

HDI° Support Center Analyst (HDI-SCA)
or HDI° Desktop Support Technician (HDI-DST)

▼

MCITP: Enterprise Desktop Support Technician 7

HDI Support Center Analyst (HDI-SCA)
Developed for professionals who provide remote support via phone, email, chat, or other contact channels, this certification focuses on strategies for effective customer care and problem resolution, the fundamentals for support processes and tools, and an introduction to ITIL processes.

HDI Desktop Support Technician (HDI-DST)
Designed specifically for those who provide desk-side support, this certification includes many of the same topics as HDI-SCA but has added components critical to in-person support such as troubleshooting and root cause analysis.

Figure I.1

The Layout of This Book

This book is recommended for those at a beginner's level with Microsoft Windows certifications all the way to a network administrator with advanced experience and previous Microsoft Professional certifications as well as experience with previous Windows versions.

If you have never made custom modifications to a Windows operating system nor have experience with modifying a registry, you shouldn't worry. You should have no problems understanding this book.

Now that we have gotten that out of the way, let's get down to how this book is constructed.

Windows 7 is Microsoft's newest operating system. There are many changes and if you are used to Microsoft XP (Not in Classic Mode) and have graduated to Vista, you will find the stepping stones to this operating system much easier. However, if you are making the jump from Windows 2000 or Windows XP in Classic Mode, some of the changes will be a difficult adjustment.

We make this book pretty easy to understand for just about everyone. We have taken the time to really understand each picture and what you are looking at. When there are multiple icons on the screen, we describe what you are looking at, and give you pointers as shown below in figure I.1, showing the alerts flag on the new Superbar. Each screenshot or picture is labeled with a description and call out to the picture. Such as this one in I.2. (Introduction.Picture Number)

Figure I.2

And also here I this example where the item we are describing is highlighted here in figure I.3.

Figure I.3

Occasionally, a screen is really cluttered and so we will point out all the significant factors of that screen as shown in figure I.4.

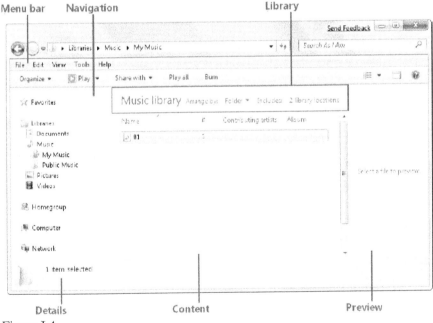

Figure I.4

Once we get past learning about the system requirements of Windows 7 in chapter 1, we will start with how the basic features are used and configured. We will the focus heavily on the more technical aspects and how to troubleshoot installations. There is actually thousands of troubleshooting recommendations from Microsoft and third parties you can perform. This book only scratches the surface of the troubleshooting techniques most likely used in business and those you will see on the exam.

Windows 7 operating system (OS) is packed with new features especially in the Enterprise and Ultimate versions such as:

- DirectAccess: Gives mobile users seamless access to corporate networks without a need to VPN.

- BranchCache: Decreases the time branch office users spend waiting to download files across the network.

- Federated Search: Find information in remote repositories, including SharePoint sites, and many others with a new simple user interface.

- BitLocker and BitLocker To Go: Helps to protect data on PCs and removable drives, with manageability to enforce encryption and backup of recovery keys.

- AppLocker: Specifies what software is allowed to run on a user's PCs through centrally managed but flexible Group Policies.

- Virtual desktop infrastructure (VDI) optimizations: Gives the user the ability to reuse virtual hard drive (VHD) images to boot a physical PC.

- Disk Imaging: Allows you to create a single OS image for deployment to users worldwide.

These are all available in the Ultimate and Enterprise versions of the software and will be discussed later in this book. But not all the features in this book are in every version. In the next chapter let's take a look at what features are available in each version, the upgrade path for legacy operating systems, and a brief description of some of the new major features of Windows 7.

Assess Yourself – Pretest

Question 1

You are the administrator of a network where all the desktops run Windows XP and are members of an Active Directory Domain Services domain. You have been tasked to migrate all the XP desktops to Windows 7 Professional. Your second task is to deploy a VPN server to support remote network access for the computers. These desktops will need to use remote access during the migration to Windows 7. What should you do?

      A. Set the VPN use port 443.

      B. Set the VPN server to CHAPv2.

      C. Configure the VPN server for 3DES encryption.

      D. Set the VPN server to Layer 2 Tunneling Protocol.

Answer: _____

Question 2

You are the administrator of a network where all the desktops run Windows 7.

The shipping department uses a Wireless Wide Area Network (WWAN), WLAN, and wired network connections to work on laptops at remote location.

The Shipping department has to reestablish their secure connections and restart multiple applications frequently. To ensure unnecessary interruption and make sure that the shipping employees are able to work what should you do?

      A. Configure each portable computer to use the VPN Reconnect feature.

      B. Create a Group Policy to configure preferred wireless access points.

      C. Configure Group Policy preferences to create multiple VPN connections.

      D. Configure each portable computer to use the Extensible Authentication Protocol.

Answer: _____

Question 3

You are the administrator of a network where all the desktops run Windows 7 and are members of an Active Directory Domain Services domain. Using the Task Manager, you discover that the memory usage on the computers is very high. You need to find the reason for the high memory usage. What should you do to determine the cause?

A. Run the Resource Monitor Tool and pay close attention to the content on the Memory tab.

B. Run the Windows Memory Management Diagnostic tool and set the memory scanning feature to graph mode.

C. In the Program Files, choose System Tools, Accessories, and then choose Memory Management Diagnostics and Configuration Tool. Run the default scan of the memory and see what is using the resources.

D. Set a user defined data set and set Memory\Available Mbytes and Memory\% Committed Bytes In Use counters.

Answer: _____

Question 4

You are the administrator of a network where all the desktops run Windows 7 and are members of an Active Directory Domain Services domain.

Several users have requested need hardware upgrades on their PC's. One of the problems noted is that their PC's randomly perform restarts automatically. After you examine one of the computers and verify the following:

- No viruses or malware.

- Only approved applications and processes are installed.

- All windows and software updates to the operating system and applications have been applied to the computer.

You need to immediately find out why the PC's are restarting automatically. What should you do?

A. Run the Boot manager log tool.

B. Run the fixmbr command from the Recovery Console.

C. Run the Windows Memory Diagnostic tool.

D. Remove the autoexec,bat to see if the problem goes away.

Answer: _____

Question 5

You are the administrator of a network where all the desktops run Windows 7 and are members of an Active Directory Domain Services domain. Your company has a policy requiring all unnecessary or unapproved services be disabled on all the computers.

The shipping department has been provided with new wireless mobile broadband adapters.

You need to make sure that computers can connect to the new broadband network. Which service should be enabled on the portable computers?

     A. WLAN AutoConfig

     B. WiFi LAN Tools

     C. The Master Browser service

     D. WWAN AutoConfig

Answer: _____

Question 6

You are the administrator of a network where all the desktops run Windows 7 and are members of an Active Directory Domain Services domain. The preview function which displays the Content view in Windows Explorer and the Search box needs to be disabled on all PC's in the company. What should you do?

     A. Go to Windows Explorer and uncheck the show snippets feature button under File Options.

     B. Set Group Policy to enable the No search results viewer.

     C. Set Group Policy to enable the Turn off the display of snippets in Content view mode setting.

     D. Set Group Policy to enable the Turn off viewer panes.

Answer: _____

Question 7

Your company has a main office and two smaller retail locations located out of state. All of the computers in your company's network all run Windows 7, connect to a Windows Server 2008 domain and are members of an Active Directory Domain Services domain. All the servers in the network environment use Windows Server 2008 R2 and are located in the main office location. Your retail office employees use a small 256K partial T1 link which is slow because of the amount of traffic and there is high latency accessing files on the network share located at the main office. You are tasked to do the following:

1. Reduce WAN link usage.

2. Lessen the latency user have when trying to accessing files at the main office.

What should you do?

> A. Configure BranchCache in Distributed Mode on a Windows Server 2008 R2 server.

> B. The BranchCache service should be configured to start automatically on a Windows 2008 Server.

> C. Change the MTU size on the server running ISA or Routing and Remote Access.

> D. Configure Quality of Service (QoS) on the Windows 2008 Server running Routing and Remote Access for the domain

Answer: _____

Question 8

All client computers on your company network run Windows 7 and are members of an Active Directory Domain Services domain. All servers in the network are running Windows Server 2008 R2 and are located in the headquarters. A remote office connects to the main office by using a cellular network.

Employees at the remote office frequently download a daily report from an IIS Web server at the main office, which causes them to incur excessive pay per bandwidth usage costs. You need to decrease the network bandwidth usage costs incurred by the remote office. What should you do?

> A. Implement Direct Access.

> B. Implement Readyboost.

> C. Implement Distributed File System.

> D. Configure Branch Cache mode.

Answer: _____

Question 9

All client computers on your company network run Windows 7 and are members of an Active Directory Domain Services domain. All the laptop users in the network connect only to the 802.1X-authenticated wireless network. Wireless settings are set through the MediaWorksPublishing.com's Group Policy.

You discover that new laptops are not able to join to the domain. What should you do to allow the computers to join the domain?

> A. Connect the portable computers to the domain by Branche Cache security authentication.
>
> B. Connect the portable computers to the wireless network by using a hidden profile.
>
> C. Connect the portable computers to the domain by using bio identification characteristics.
>
> D. Connect the portable computers to the wireless network by using a Bootstrap Profile.

Answer: _____

Question 10

All client computers on your company network run Windows 7 and are members of an Active Directory Domain Services domain. All servers in the network are running Windows Server 2008 R2. Employees use a VPN connection to connect to the company's headquarters from a remote location.

Employees remain connected to the VPN server to browse the Internet, even for personal use. This is becoming an issue and you are instructed to make sure that remote users cannot use the Internet while connected to the VPN. What should you do?

> A. Configure the VPN connection eliminating all DNS entries.
>
> B. Configure the DHCP to stop assigning IP addresses when connecting through the VPN.
>
> C. Use Group Policy to disable the Use default gateway on remote network setting on each client computer.
>
> D. Use Group Policy to block port 80 on the firewall on each computer connecting through the VPN.

Answer: _____

Question 11

All of the computers in your company's network all run Windows 7 and connect to a Windows Server 2008 domain. You plan to use Group Policy to enable BitLocker Drive Encryption (BDE) with the following requirements:

1. The BitLocker recovery keys are stored in a single centralized location. ·

2. All data is encrypted but only after a backup of the recovery key is available.

Which of the following should be done?

A. BitLocker /keystore command from a Command Prompt.

B. Using the BitLocker Wizard choose the Default Folder option for secure password storage and identify the location the shared keys should be stored.

C. From the Action menu option choose Enable BitLocker encrypted drive recovery key. Then replace the default local drive selection with a secure network share.

D. Use the Active Directory Domain Services setting to enable the Store BitLocker recovery information.

Answer: _____

Question 12

There is an Active Directory domain and a Direct Access infrastructure already configured in your network. Windows 7 is installed on a new laptop and you have joined the computer to the domain. You have to make sure that the computer can establish DirectAccess connections. Which of the following should be performed?

A. Create Network Discovery firewall exception should be enabled.

B. Add the users to the Remote Operators group.

C. Create a VPN connection new network connection should be created.

D. Install a valid computer certificate.

Answer: _____

Question 13

All client computers on your company network run Windows 7 and are members of an Active Directory Domain Services domain. Employees use Windows Internet Explorer 8 to access the Internet. Users believe that their computers are infected with malicious software which you soon confirm. As the network administrator you are tasked to configure the settings in Internet Explorer 8 to prevent malicious software from being installed on the computers. What should you do?

    A. Configure Popup Blocker.

    B. Configure SmartScreen Filter.

    C. Restrict access to the Local intranet zone.

    D. Implement a content filter on the firewall.

Answer: _____

Question 14

You use a laptop named Laptop1 which runs Windows 7. There is a Windows 2008 R2 server named Server1 that contains a shared folder named Data. You need to configure Laptop1 to cache and encrypt the files from the Data share so they can be used when Laptop1 is not connected to the network. You want the files in the Data share to automatically synch each time Laptop1 connects to the network. Which action should be performed?

    A. On Server1, the files should be encrypted on the Data share. Copy the data to a folder on the Laptop1.

    B. Copy the files from the Data share to the Documents library and turn on BitLocker To Go Drive Encryption.

    C. You should make the Data share available offline and enable encryption of offline files on Laptop1.

    D. BitLocker Drive Encryption should be configured on Server1. You should make Data share available offline on all computers in the network.

Answer: _____

Question 15

All client computers on your company network run Windows 7 and are members of an Active Directory Domain Services domain. Employees using laptops report that they get connected to a public wireless network from the company conference room.

You need to ensure that the employees connect to the company wireless network by default from anywhere within the company premises.

What should you do?

> A. Configure the Network authentication setting to allow MAC authentication.
>
> B. Rename your wireless SSID with starting with an "A" so it falls before the public wireless networks SSID.
>
> C. Apply a Wireless Network Policy to set the company wireless network as the preferred network.
>
> D. Apply a Group Policy to allow only the network SSID.

Answer: _____

Question 16

You have two computers named Laptop1 and Computer2. Windows Vista is run on Laptop1. Windows 7 is run on Computer2. You are tasked with migrating all the users files and profiles from Laptop1 to Computer2. Which command would be used to identify how much space is required to complete the migration?

> A. Run Windows Easy Migrate and press test the C: drive on Laptop1.
>
> B. dsmigrate \\Laptop1\store /nocompress /p should be run on Computer2.
>
> C. loadstate \\Laptop1\store /nocompress should be run on Computer2.
>
> D. scanstate c:\store /nocompress /p should be run on Laptop1.

Answer: _____

Question 17

All client computers on your company network run Windows 7 and are members of an Active Directory Domain Services domain. All servers in the network are running Windows Server 2008 R2. You need to ensure that data stored on removable drives is encrypted. What should you do?

A. Set the Removable Disks:Apply only BitLocker encryption.

B. Set the Control use of BitLocker on removable drives option to Allow users to apply BitLocker on removable drives by using Group Policy.

C. Set Group Policy to enable Configure use of passwords for removable data drives

Answer: _____

Question 18

You have a workgroup which contains seven computers running Windows 7 Professional. A computer named Computer1 has MP4 files to share. What should Computer 1, do to share the files? (Choose 2.)

A. Connect a removable drive and enable BitLocker To Go.

B. Create a Homegroup with a shared password.

C. All BranchCache rules should be enabled in Windows Firewall.

D. The files should be moved to a Media Library.

Answer: _____

Question 19

The Aero Shake feature will work if which of the following conditions are met? (Choose 2.)

A. A display adapter compatible with WDDM is installed.

B. Aero features are downloaded from Microsoft.

C. The windows experience index is at least 2.

D. The Windows Experience Index is 3 or greater.

Answer: _____

Question 20

All client computers on your company network run Windows 7 and are members of an Active Directory Domain Services domain. All computers are configured to automatically download and install Windows updates. You are the network administrator of a network which requires a proxy server for access to the Internet but does not use the Web Proxy Auto-Discovery (WPAD).

Another network technician notices that none of the networks computers are receiving installed updates. What should you do to fix the issue and allow the computers to automatically install updates?

> A. Set Automatic Updates to install through WSUS.
>
> B. Set Automatic Updates to override proxy settings and use an administrator account.
>
> C. Run the proxycfg.exe tool on each computer on the network segment.
>
> D. Log on to each computer on the network segment as Administrator and configure an Internet Explorer proxy manually.

Answer: _____

Question 21

All client computers on your company network run Windows 7 and are members of an Active Directory Domain Services domain. Employees access websites each day by using Windows Internet Explorer 8. As the network administrator you notice employees are accessing restricted websites, by modifying the security levels assigned to Internet zones. Your supervisor wants you to stop employees from modifying the security levels. What should you do?

> A. Disable the Protected Security Group Policy setting for Internet Explorer.
>
> B. Disable the Zone Elevation Protection Group Policy setting.
>
> C. Modify the Group Policy option and enable the Zone Elevation Protection setting.
>
> D. Enable the Group Policy setting called Do Not allow user to enable users from modifying Internet Explorer Policies.

Answer: _____

Question 22

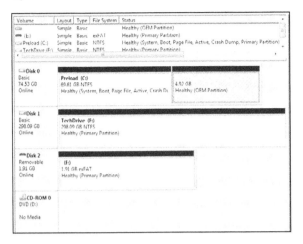

You have a computer that runs Windows 7. You open the Disk Management in the Computer Management MMC. You need to make sure that you are able to create a new partition on Disk 0 but the space is used. Which of the following would allow you to make another partition on Disk 0, as shown in the figure above?

> A. Create a Virtual Hard Disk (VHD) and assign as Disk 0. Change Disk 0 to Disk 3.
>
> B. In order to make sure of this, volume C should be compressed.
>
> C. In order to make sure of this, Disk 0 should be converted into a dynamic disk.
>
> D. Shrink volume C to make space for another volume.

Answer: _____

Question 23

All client computers on your company network run Windows 7 and are members of an Active Directory Domain Services domain. Employees log on to their computers as Standard users. A malicious software attack is affecting your network users. Many users are receiving User Account Control (UAC) messages frequently requesting permission to elevate privileges. You know that the malicious software attack is responsible for these UAC prompts and need to ensure that employees are unable to provide elevated credentials. Which of the following should you do?

A. Configure the Group Policy User Account Control to enable the UAC only elevate for Administrator logins.

B. Configure the Group Policy User Account Control to enable the "Secure desktop for Standard users prompt."

C. Configure the Group Policy User Account Control: called "Behavior of the elevation prompt for standard users setting to automatically deny elevation requests."

D. Turn off the UAC prompt by modifying each computers security settings in the Control panel.

Answer: _____

Question 24

There is an Active Directory domain in your network. There are two computers which have already joined the domain named Computer1 and Computer 2 running Windows 7 Professional. From Computer 1, you can recover all *Encrypting File System (EFS)* encrypted files for users in the domain. You have to make sure that you can recover all EFS encrypted files from Computer 2. What action should you perform?

A. Use the Cipher.exe /wc:\. The take the certificate and place it on Computer 2 to be able to read the encrypted files.

B. Use AppLocker to create a data recovery certificate on Computer1 and copy the certificate to Computer2.

C. Export the data using the new Windows 7 EFS Recovery tool using the /export syntax on Computer 1 and using the /target syntax for Computer 2.

D. Export the Data Recovery Agent Certificate on Computer 1 to Computer 2.

Answer: _____

Question 25

All client computers on your company network run Windows 7 and are members of an Active Directory Domain Services domain. All servers in the network are running Windows Server 2008 R2.

You are finding that someone has a burned CD that has a virus that is installing automatically. You need to ensure that virus does not automatically run on the computers. What should you do to fix this?

     A. Disable the Windows Installer service from the Domain Controller.

     B. Use Group policy and enable the "Disable the Autoplay function".

     C. Set the auto SHIFT press for CD's configured in a Active Directory domain script.

     D. Prevent the installation of unsigned applications by requiring a certificate by enabling the Security Certificate service on the server.

Answer: _____

Question 26

After the installation of third-party software you find the Original Equipment Manufacturer (OEM) recovery partition is no longer installed on the PC. The Boot Configuration Database (BCD) has also been corrupted. You need to repair the BCD so that the computers can boot up. What should you do?

     A. Create a new system repair disc and run the Startup Repair recovery tool.

     B. Run the System Image Recovery tool from the Windows 7 Professional or the Windows 7 Ultimate DVD.

     C. Select the Last Known Good Configuration after booting the PC.

     D. You will need to reinstall Windows 7 to replace the BCD.

Answer: _____

Question 27

All client computers on your company network run Windows 7 and are members of an Active Directory Domain Services domain. The shipping department staffs run an application that collects data from 09:30 hours to 15:00 hours every day to transmit shipping information. After the data collection, the application generates reports from the information.

While the PC is generating reports, the shipping department staff experience slow performance on their computers. You discover that the usage of the processor on the computer is between 85 and 100 percent. What should you do to increase the speed of the PC's during the generation of the reports?

    A. Add a USB processor.

    B. Use Virtual Server to offset some of the processing on the CPU.

    C. Add more RAM to buffer the waiting data to the CPU.

    D. Set the priority of the application to Low.

Answer: _____

Question 28

All client computers on your company network run Windows 7 and are members of an Active Directory Domain Services domain. The shipping employees run an application that generates large reports. These reports take too long to generate on the computers. You want to confirm that processor time and memory are acceptable and identify why these reports are generating slowly. If you create a User Defined Data Collector Set which of the following variable information should you collect?

    A. Process\% Privileged Time and Process\% User Time counters for each processor core

    B. Physical Disk\ Avg. Disk Queue Length and Physical Disk\% Disk Time counters for Disk0 of the Computers

    C. Logical Disk\Free Megabytes and Logical Disk\% Free Space counters for the user data drives of the computers

    D. Memory\Available Mbytes and Memory\% Committed Bytes In Use counters

Answer: _____

Question 29

In Windows 7 you can control when users such as kids can login to Windows 7. Which of the following best describes where to configure this option?

A. You cannot choose this feature unless you are connected to a domain.

B. Go to the Start, Control Panel, User Accounts and Family Safety, Setup Parental Controls, and then choose Time Restrictions.

C. Go to Start, Control Panel. User Profiles, and then Time Restriction Settings.

D. Go to the Homegroup settings and choose Offline Time Settings.

Answer: _____

Question 30

All client computers on your company network run Windows 7 and are members of an Active Directory Domain Services domain. Each computer has four 1-GB RAM modules and a single physical disk.

When the employees run a three-dimensional (3-D) design application that extensively uses the RAM, they experience slow performance on their computers. You discover that the swap files on the computers are extensively used. What should you do to fix the issue?

A. Disable the hardware acceleration on the monitor card.

B. Increase the RAM to 8 GB.

C. Add a second disk to decrease paging

D. Configure the virtual memory on the computers so that the initial size of the virtual memory is equal to the maximum size of the virtual memory.

Answer: _____

Question 31

All client computers on your company network run Windows 7 and are members of an Active Directory Domain Services domain. All servers in the network are running Windows Server 2008 R2. The Active Directory Domain Services domain name is mediaworkspublishing.com. Employees access the company intranet using the URL of http:// sharing mediaworkspublishing.com.

Which of the following will allow a single user to access the URL of http://sharing.mediaworkspublishing.com and allow them to see a different server so he can access a new version of the site without affecting other employees' access to the current site??

    A. Add an entry to the Hosts file that specifies sharing.mediaworkspublishing.com and the IP address of the new server on the employee's computer.

    B. Create a sub DNS domain and record for sharing.mediaworksublishing.com that specifies the IP address of the test server.

    C. Use Group Policy to restrict the user from the original server and then use the ROUTEPRINT command to map the new IP address for the server.

    D. All of the above will work.

    Answer: _____

Question 32

All client computers on your company network run Windows 7 and are members of an Active Directory Domain Services domain. You deploy network printers. You need to ensure that employees are able to find these printers. What should you do first?

    A. Check to make sure that your print servers include 64-bit Windows 7 print drivers.

    B. Enter the printers IP in the Location Aware Printing utility.

    C. Create a group policy to enable the "Automatically publish new printers."

    D. Do nothing. Printer will automatically appear on all PC's that join the domain as long as they are installed on the domain controller.

    Answer: _____

Question 33

To establish a DirectAccess connection to the network, what is the first requirement?

A. Install a certificate

B. Create a VPN connection

C. A static IPv4 address

D. A static IPv6 address

Answer: _____

Question 34

You are the network administrator of a network that has client computers that run Windows 7 and other client computers that run Windows XP Professional. After enabling the Network Discovery feature on the Windows 7 computers you find that the Windows XP computers do not appear on the created network map. What should you do to make them appear on the map?

A. Place the XP computer names in the Computers folder in 'Active Directory.

B. Install the Link Layer Topology Discovery (LLTD) Responder on the Windows XP computers.

C. Add the XP computer names Network Discovery search feature.

C. Map at least one share from the domain controllers on each XP computer.

Answer: _____

Question 35

All client computers on your company network run Windows 7 and are members of an Active Directory Domain Services domain using Windows 2008 R2 servers. Another network administrator changes the IP address of an application server and employees are unable to connect to the server after the change. You need to ensure that the employees are able to connect to the server immediately. Which of the following is the correct fix for the problem?

A. Use the "net send *" command to send a message to all users instructing them to open the server from its IP address.

B. Email each user a new Hosts file.

C. Run a remote Windows PowerShell script to flush the DNS resolver cache on each computer.

D. Email each user instructions to use

Answer: _____

Question 36

To audit the usage of other users on a shared folder on your Windows 7 computer, which of the following actions should be taken?

A. Configure the Audit object access setting in the local Group Policy.

B. Right click on the folder being shared and choose the Audit directory service Access setting.

C. In the Event Viewer, right click on the System Log. Choose Properties and select all the options for logging including folder access.

D. Modify the properties of the Security log from the Event Viewer.

Answer: _____

Question 37

You are in charge of a computer that runs Windows 7. You find that an application named Google Desktop runs during the startup process. You have to prevent only Google Desktop from running during the startup process. Users must be allowed to run Google Desktop manually however. What is the proper way to configure this without using third party tools?

A. The msconfig.exe tool should be modified.

B. The application control policy should be modified from the local Group Policy.

C. The software boot policy should be modified from the local Group Policy.

D. The Startup applications in the System Configuration tool should be modified.

Answer: _____

Question 38

You have a Virtual Hard Disk (VHD) with Windows 7 installed and a computer running Windows 7 Ultimate. Which procedure of the following would allow you to book the Windows 7 PC from the VHD?

A. Run bcdedit.exe and modify the Windows Boot Manager.

B. Select vdisk should be run from Diskpart.exe.

C. Modify the BIOS to boot from an ISO.

D. Press F12 at startup and wait for the option to press any key to start from a VHD.

Answer: _____

Question 39

Which of the following is used to control when the security pop-up notifications are used?

    A. Security Control Manager

    B. User Account Control

    C. User Access Control Panel

    D. Notification Control Settings Manager

Answer: _____

Question 32

Which of the following is not a Windows PE tool?

    A. Diskpart

    B. Drvload

    C. Oscdimg

    D. Winpeshl

    E. None of the above.

Answer: _____

Question 40

All 260 client computers on your company network run Windows 7 and are members of an Active Directory Domain Services domain. Your team consists of 20 desktop support technicians who are sent to resolve a hardware issue with a user's computer. Both technicians troubleshoot but get different results by using their own User Defined Data Collector Sets. In order to standardize the Data Collector Set on a network share that is accessible to your team which of the following should you perform?

A. Create an Event Trace Data Collector Set

B. Create a Performance Counter Data Collector Set

C. Create a Performance Counter Alert Data Collector Set Template

D. Create a System Configuration Information Data Collector Set Template

Answer: _____

Question 41

Which of the following can be used to increase the physical memory on your Windows 7 PC and increase the speed?

A. PhysiRAM

B. Aero Glass

C. DirectAccess

D: ReadyBoost

Answer: _____

Question 42

A USB external drive is attached to a Windows 7 Professional computer. You want to enable BitLocker To Go on the USB disk. Which of the following must be done?

A. In order to make sure of this, obtain a client certificate from an enterprise certification authority (CA).

B. You must install the Encrypting File System (EFS) from the Add/Remove Windows Components.

C. In order to make sure of this, the computer should be upgraded to Windows 7 Ultimate or Windows 7 Enterprise.

D. You need to download BitLocker To Go from Microsoft's website.

Answer: _____

Question: 43

All client computers on your company network run Windows 7 and are members of an Active Directory Domain Services domain. All servers in the network are running Windows Server 2008 R2. The shipping department staff are all currently local administrators on their computers and are members of the Shipping Global Security Group. A new version of the shipping software application is available on the network.

As the network administrator you are tasked to apply an AppLocker security policy to the Shipping Global Security Group. You need to ensure that members of the Shipping Group are not allowed to upgrade the software on their computers by doing which of the following?

A. Create an Enforce rule restriction based on the version of the software.

B. Move the users to the No Software Install Rights Active Directory Group.

C. Create a certificate with only Enterprise Administrator rights.

D. Create an Enforce rule restriction based on the publisher of the software.

Answer: _____

Question 44

All client computers on your company network run Windows 7 and are members of an Active Directory Domain Services domain. The application control method was established by using Software Restriction Policies. These Software Restriction Policies were deployed in a single Group Policy object (GPO) linked to the Organizational Unit (OU) that contains the computers.

You plan to deploy Microsoft Office 2007 Professional and configure AppLocker for control within the GPO. To ensure that core business applications continue to function, which of the following should be done?

    A. Create AppLocker rules and apply them to the Certificate Policy.

    B. Move the AppLocker rules to a different GPO.

    C. Create a new GPO. Apply the Software Restriction Policy and the AppLocker rules to the new GPO.

    D. Create a new AppLocker rules allowing for only digitally signed certificates.

Answer: _____

Question 45

All client computers on your company network run Windows 7. A standard Windows 7 image is loaded on all new computers on the network. Some of the users are complaining that the pen interface is not working on their new tablet PC's. Which of the following will most likely resolve the user's issues?

    A. Turn on the Media Features.

    B. Turn on the Tablet PC Components.

    C. Turn off the keyboard and start the pen service.

    D. Turn on OCR Mode.

Answer: _____

Question: 46

All client computers on your company network run Windows 7 and are members of an Active Directory Domain Services domain. All client computers on your company network were recently migrated from Windows XP to Windows 7. The company however uses a custom designed application that is currently not compatible with Windows 7. A shim has been created and applied to eliminate compatibility issues until the software can be made compatible with Windows 7. The developers have given you a security update for the custom application. However, during testing you are unable to install the application. You as the network administrator need to ensure that the application can be installed in the test environment before it can be deployed to the production environment. Which of the following should be performed?

    A. Modify the shim to apply to all versions of the application.

    B. Place and exception so there are no UAC prompts.

    C. Run the .msi file from an elevated command prompt.

    D. Modify the shim to apply only to the new version of the application.

Answer: _____

Question 47

What action would you perform to prevent Internet Explorer from saving any data during a browsing session?

    A. The security settings for the Internet zone should be disabled.

    B. The BranchCache service should be disabled.

    C. The InPrivate Blocking list should be disabled.

    D. Open an InPrivate Browsing session in IE.

Answer: _____

Question 48

All client computers on your company network run Windows 7 and are members of an Active Directory Domain. AppLocker is configured to allow only approved applications to run. Employees with Standard user account permissions are able to run applications that install into the user profile folder. What should you do as the administrator to stop unauthorized applications from being installed?

A. Create Executable Rules by selecting the Create Default Rules option.

B. Create Windows Installer Rules by selecting in Group Policy

C. Create the following Windows Installer Rule: Deny – Everyone - %OSDRIVE%\Users\<user name>\Downloads* -No

D. Go to each PC and remove the local administrator account from the local PC's Administrator Group.

Answer: _____

Question 49

You are in charge of two computers that running Windows 7 called Computer1 and Computer 2. What action should you perform to make sure you can remotely execute commands on Computer02 from Computer01?

A. You should enable Windows Remote Management (WinRM) in the Control Panel on both computers.

B. winrm quickconfig should be run on C01.

C. You should enable Windows Remote Management (WinRM) from the Windows 2008 R2 server in the network

D. winrm quickconfig should be run on C02.

Answer: _____

Question 50

All client computers on your company network run Windows 7. Several legacy software applications are made available on the computers by using Windows XP Mode (XPM). Employees report that all Start menu shortcuts for the legacy applications are missing from their computers. Which of the following is the correct way to allow all the legacy shortcuts to be accessible from the Start menu?

> A. Enable the Auto Publish option for Virtual Machine Settings on the Windows 7 computers.
>
> B. Copy the program shortcuts to the Start menu of the Windows 7 computers.
>
> C. Reinstall the applications on the XPM machines on all the Windows 7 computers.
>
> D. All of the above will work.

Answer: _____

Question 51

All client computers on your company network run Windows 7.

An application has stopped working. The application is dependent on a service that runs automatically and logs on to the domain by using a dedicated service account. You also discover that an entry in the event log has the following message: "Logon failure: unknown user name or bad password." You need to ensure that the service runs successfully. What should you do?

> A. Add the dedicated account to the local Administrators group.
>
> B. Add the employee user account to the local Administrators group.
>
> C. Reset the employee password and configure it to never expire.
>
> D. Reset the service account password and configure it to never expire.

Answer: D

> Answer: _____

Question: 52

You manage a computer that runs Windows 7. Good thing you imaged your PC after you installed Windows 7, because a virus has infected your PC. Which of the following procedures will allow you to restore your PC?

A. Restart computer should be started from Windows Preinstallation Environment (Windows PE) and then ImageLoader.exe should be run.

B. Use the Last Known Good Configuration feature to start the computer.

C. Boot the computer from the Windows 7 DVD and then the Startup Repair tools. Choose system repair using an image.

D. Boot the computer from the Windows 7 DVD and then choose the System Image Recovery tool.

Answer: _____

Question 53

All client computers on your company network run Windows 7 and are members of an Active Directory Domain. All servers in the network are running Windows 2003. After a user attempts to log on to the domain from his computer, he receives the following error message:

> *"System cannot log you on to the domain because the system's computer account in its primary domain is missing or the password on that account is incorrect."*

Which of the following is the correct way to resolve the issue?

A. Change the user's password.

B. Reset the users GUID on the domain controller.

C. Add the user account of the employee to the Enterprise Administrators group.

D. Remove the computer from the domain, place it in a workgroup and then re-add the computer again to the domain.

Answer: _____

Question 54

All client computers on your company network run Windows 7 and are members of an Active Directory Domain Services domain. All servers in the network are running Windows Server 2008 R2. You suspect that a device listed under Non-Plug and Play Drivers in the Device Manager is causing problems. How do you immediately stop the device to determine if the device is the cause?

A. Open the device Properties dialog box in Device Manager. On the Driver tab, change the USB Start Type to Disabled.

B. Open the device Properties dialog box in Device Manager. On the Driver tab, click Stop.

C. Open the device Properties dialog box in Device Manager. On the USB Driver tab, click Disable.

D. Open the device Properties dialog box in Device Manager. On the Driver tab, click Uninstall.

Answer: _____

Question 55

There are multiple users that log on to a Windows 7 Professional computer. You need to deny one user access to removable devices on the computer. All other users must have access to the removable drives. What action should you perform?

A. The settings of all removable devices should be modified from Device Manager.

B. An application control policy should be modified from the local Group Policy.

C. A removable storage access policy should be modified from the local Group Policy.

D. The BitLocker Drive Encryption settings should be modified from Control Panel.

Answer: _____

Question 56

You use a computer that runs Windows 7 Ultimate. You are asked to prevent users from copying unencrypted files to removable drives. What action should you perform?

A. The Trusted Platform System (TPS) settings should be modified from a local Group Policy.

B. TPS should be initialized from the Trusted Platform Settings (TPM) snap-in.

C. The BitLocker Drive Encryption settings should be modified from Control Panel.

D. The BitLocker Drive Encryption settings should be modified from a local Group Policy.

Answer: _____

Question 57

There is a head office and a branch office in your company network. The branch office has computers that run Windows 7 Professional. A network administrator enables BranchCache in the head office. You have to make sure that other computers in the branch office can access the cached content on your computer. So what action should be performed?

A. The Windows Firewall, Advanced Security rules should be modified.

B. Turn on Internet Information Services (IIS).

C. The computer should be configured as a hosted cache client.

D. The BranchCache service should be configured to start automatically on a Windows 2003 server.

Answer: _____

Question 58

All client computers on your company network run Windows 7 and are members of an Active Directory Domain Services domain. The event logs contain errors from an application source as well as the Kernel-Power source. You plan to track these errors to help troubleshoot the problem. To capture only the relevant data to generate a report which of the following should you do?

A. Open Event Viewer and sort by "Source = CRITICAL" only.

B. Open Event Viewer and create a Custom View. Include the application and system logs and include the event sources. Save the filter results as an XML file.

C. Open Event Viewer, go to Properties and create a filter.

D. Use Performance Monitor to create a template EventLog-Application Event Session.

Answer: _____

Question 59

All client computers on your company network run Windows 7 and are members of an Active Directory Domain Services domain. An employee installs several new applications on a computer but notices the computer takes much longer to startup after he logs in. What tool can be used to reduce the startup time?

A. Run the Sysedit command.

B. Use the Startup console to eliminate startup items.

C. Use the Task Manager tool to stop the services.

D. Run the msconfig tool.

Answer: _____

Questions 60

Which of the following permissions are automatically set on a file when you apply the Read & Execute (Deny) NTFS permission? (Choose 2)

A. List Folder Contents (Deny)

B. Modify (Deny)

C. Write (Deny)

D. Read (Deny)

Answer: _____

Chapter 1 – Upgrade Paths, Requirements and Migration Strategies

Windows 7 Starter, Home Basic, Home Premium, Professional, Enterprise and Ultimate, along with the N versions for the European market each represent a simplification over the equivalent Vista versions that came out in January of 2007.

In Windows 7 each version is a superset of one another. If you upgrade from one version to the next, they keep all features and functionality from the previous edition. For example moving from Starter to Ultimate, each edition will supersede the previous, containing all of its features and adding additional components.

Microsoft is initially focused on the marketing and distribution of Windows 7 Home Premium,, Windows 7 Professional, and Windows 7 Ultimate. Rather than pushing all editions on the market at once, Microsoft is aiming the core editions at specific market segments to try and simplify the choices for consumers.

> *Alert:* One of the biggest mistakes made by those who purchased Vista was that they didn't realize you could not join an Active Directory domain using any Home Edition, Starter Edition, or Media Center Editions of Vista. The same is true for Windows 7 versions as well.

Although Figure 1.1 on the next page only shows three products, there are actually seven Windows 7 Editions: Starter, Home Basic, Home Premium, Professional, Enterprise and Ultimate.

> **NOTE:** *You can get the current Windows 7 comparison matrix from Microsoft's website:* http://www.Microsoft.com/windows/windows-7/compare-editions/default.aspx

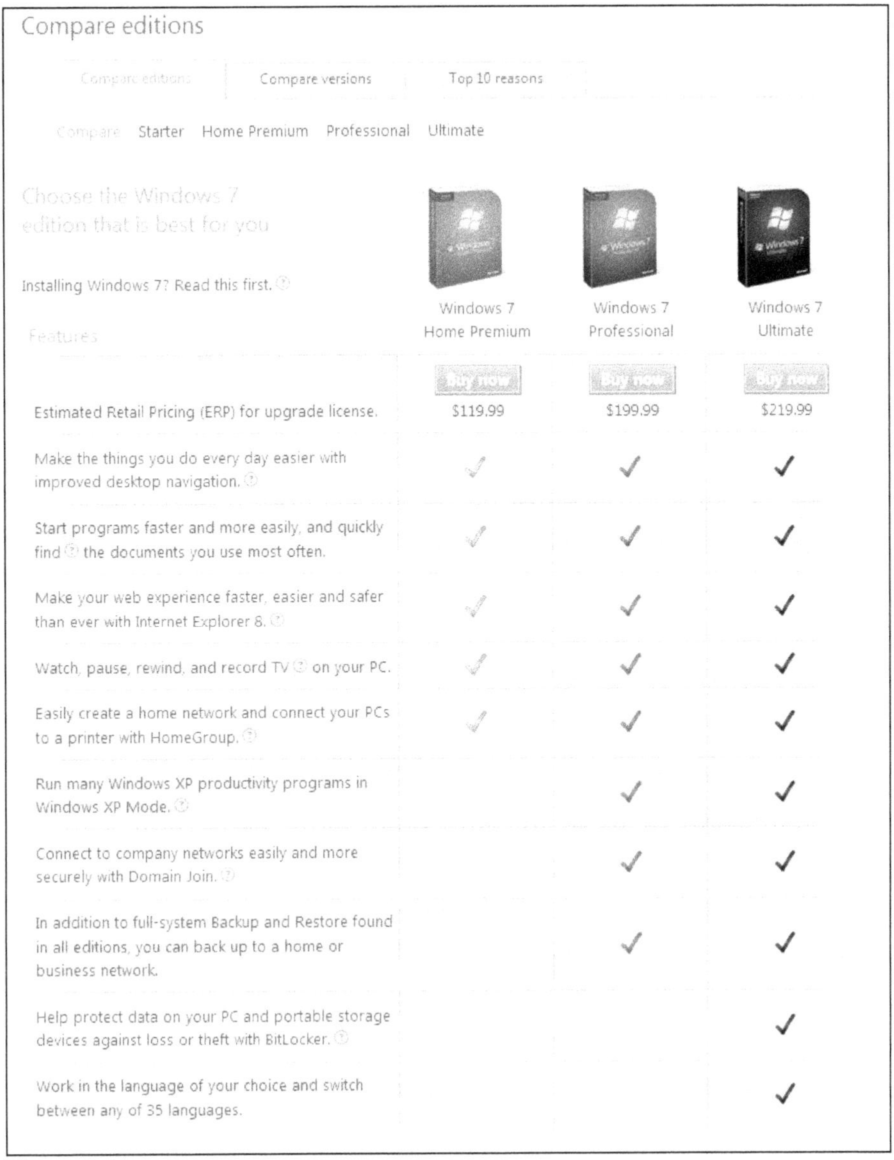

Compare editions | Compare versions | Top 10 reasons

Compare | Starter | Home Premium | Professional | Ultimate

Choose the Windows 7
edition that is best for you

Installing Windows 7? Read this first. ⑦

Features

	Windows 7 Home Premium	Windows 7 Professional	Windows 7 Ultimate
	Buy now	Buy now	Buy now
Estimated Retail Pricing (ERP) for upgrade license.	$119.99	$199.99	$219.99
Make the things you do every day easier with improved desktop navigation. ⑦	✓	✓	✓
Start programs faster and more easily, and quickly find ⑦ the documents you use most often.	✓	✓	✓
Make your web experience faster, easier and safer than ever with Internet Explorer 8. ⑦	✓	✓	✓
Watch, pause, rewind, and record TV ⑦ on your PC.	✓	✓	✓
Easily create a home network and connect your PCs to a printer with HomeGroup. ⑦	✓	✓	✓
Run many Windows XP productivity programs in Windows XP Mode. ⑦		✓	✓
Connect to company networks easily and more securely with Domain Join. ⑦		✓	✓
In addition to full-system Backup and Restore found in all editions, you can back up to a home or business network.		✓	✓
Help protect data on your PC and portable storage devices against loss or theft with BitLocker. ⑦			✓
Work in the language of your choice and switch between any of 35 languages.			✓

Figure 1.1

The prices in Figure 1.1 represent the upgrade price from another Windows desktop operating system. The prices in Figure 1.2 are for the full versions of the Windows 7 for new PC's.

Figure 1.2

Windows 7 Editions

Windows 7 is designed to run on a very broad set of hardware, from small-notebook PCs to full gaming desktops. This way, customers can install the version of Windows 7 they want regardless of the hardware they already have.

Many people have Vista and XP and only want to upgrade to the equivalent version of what they currently have. So let us take a look at the different XP and Vista versions and match them up to the Windows 7 equivalent. We will also look at the availability (How you can obtain that version?), and the Windows 7 key features.

Windows 7 Starter

The equivalent of Windows Vista Starter and Windows XP Starter editions.

Availability: Worldwide, however this version is only pre-installed on new PCs by an OEM (original equipment manufacturer).

Features: Superbar (evolved taskbar), Jump Lists, Windows Media Player, Backup and Restore capabilities, Action Center, Device Stage, Play To, Fax and Scan, Games.

Windows 7 key features: Windows Media Center, Live Thumbnail previews, Home Group, users are limited to running only three concurrent applications.

Windows 7 Home Basic

The equivalent of Windows Vista Basic and Windows XP Home Edition.

Availability: Exclusively for emerging markets, only pre-installed on new PCs by an OEM (original equipment manufacturer).

Features: Superbar (evolved taskbar), Jump Lists, Windows Media Player, Backup and Restore capabilities, Action Center, Device Stage, Play To, Fax and Scan, Games.

Windows 7 key features: Aero Glass GUI, Live Thumbnail Previews, Internet Connection Sharing, Windows Media Center.

Windows 7 Home Premium

The equivalent of Windows Vista Home Premium and of Windows XP Media Center

Availability: Worldwide via mainstream retail resellers and OEM channels.

Windows 7 key features: Aero Glass GUI, Aero Background, Aero Peek, Aero Snap, Live Thumbnail previews, Multi Touch capabilities, Home Group, Windows Media Center, DVD playback and authoring, Premium Games, Mobility Center.

Cut Win 7 key features: Domain join, Remote Desktop host, Advanced Backup, EFS, Offline Folders

Windows 7 Professional

The equivalent of Windows Vista Business and Windows XP Professional.

Availability: Worldwide via mainstream retail resellers and OEM channels.

Features: Aero Glass GUI, Aero Background, Aero Peek, Aero Snap, Live Thumbnail previews, Multi Touch capabilities, Home Group, Windows Media Center, DVD playback and authoring, Premium Games, Mobility Center, Domain join, Remote Desktop host, Location Aware printing, EFS, Mobility Center, Presentation Mode, Offline Folders.

Windows 7 key features: BitLocker, BitLocker To Go, AppLocker, Direct Access, Branche Cache, MUI language packs, and boot from VHD.

Windows 7 Enterprise/Ultimate

The equivalent of Windows Vista Enterprise or Vista Ultimate.

Availability: Worldwide, but only to Microsoft's Software Assurance (SA) customers via Volume Licensing.

Features: Aero Glass GUI, Aero Background, Aero Peek, Aero Snap, Live Thumbnail previews, Multi Touch capabilities, Home Group, Windows Media Center, DVD playback and authoring, Premium Games, Mobility Center, Domain join, Remote Desktop host, Location Aware printing, EFS, Mobility Center, Presentation Mode, Offline Folders, BitLocker, BitLocker To Go, AppLocker, Direct Access, Branche Cache, MUI language packs, and boot from VHD.

Windows 7 key features: Windows 7 Enterprise contains all the features offered in Ultimate but is available only to businesses buying in volume.

Upgrade Paths

Unfortunately, because of features and compatibility issues, only a limited number of versions can be used as an upgrade path for newer versions. Attempting to upgrade a 32-bit(x86) operating system to a 64-bit(x64) operating system and vice versa will always require a complete reinstall.

Upgrading from Windows Vista to Windows 7

This is a tough pill to swallow for those who upgraded to Vista right away when it first hit the market. The RTM(Release to Manufacturing) edition of Windows Vista (the one released at the end of January 2007) won't have the option of upgrading to Windows 7. Microsoft's documentation indicates that upgrades to Windows 7 are supported only for Vista Service Pack 1 and SP2 editions.

When it comes down to Vista-to-Windows 7 upgrades, "Cross-architecture in-place upgrades (for example, x86 to x64) are not supported. Cross-language in-place upgrades (for example, en-us to de-de) are not supported. Cross-media type in-place upgrades (for example, Staged to Unstaged or Unstaged to Staged) are also not supported.

Let us now list all the remaining versions and whether an upgrade is available:

- No upgrade path for Windows Vista Starter (SP1, SP2), not even to Windows 7 Starter.

- Windows Vista Home Basic (SP1, SP2) 32-bit (x86) and 64-bit (x64) can be upgraded to Windows 7 Home Basic, Home Premium and Ultimate 32-bit (x86) and 64-bit (x64).

- Windows Vista Home Premium (SP1, SP2) 32-bit (x86) and 64-bit (x64) can be upgraded to Windows 7 Home Premium and Ultimate 32-bit (x86) and 64-bit (x64).

- Windows Vista Business (SP1, SP2) 32-bit (x86) and 64-bit (x64) can be upgraded to Windows 7 Professional, Enterprise and Ultimate 32-bit (x86) and 64-bit (x64);

- Windows Vista Enterprise (SP1, SP2) 32-bit (x86) and 64-bit (x64) can be upgraded to Windows 7 Enterprise 32-bit (x86) and 64-bit (x64);

- Windows Vista Ultimate (SP1, SP2) 32-bit (x86) and 64-bit (x64) can be upgraded to Windows 7 Ultimate 32-bit (x86) and 64-bit (x64);

- No upgrade path for Windows Vista Home Basic N (SP1, SP2), not even to Windows 7 N or E;

- No upgrade path for Windows Vista Business N (SP1, SP2), not even to Windows 7 N or E.

- No upgrade path exists for Windows XP, 2000, NT, ME, or 98.

Improvements over Vista

The prospect of migrating an entire company to a new operating system is almost always a daunting venture. You'll need to make sure you get a return on the significant investment that you'll make in the product itself. The staff, time and resources needed to install it and work out the inevitable kinks.

Windows 7 has changed the name, look, feel, features, speed, and even the logo's to part ways with Vista because of the bad vibes that still resonate. Windows Vista met with almost immediate critical disapproval when it was released in January 2007. To be fair, Vista had many improvements over the XP operating system, including better security, file sharing, and search capabilities. But those were largely overshadowed by its shortcomings: constant security pop ups, excessive use of RAM, an overly aggressive User Account Control (UAC) feature, hardware incompatibility, and more.

Now comes Windows 7 and if the early reviews are any gauge including my review, Microsoft appears to have ironed out many of the issues that haunted Vista. In fact, some reviewers including myself feel it is the best Microsoft Operating System ever produced.

Improved security

Security is always a big issue with Windows. Witness the flurry of activity and tension that surrounds the typical Patch Tuesday. Windows 7 addresses the issue with a number of security upgrades. Microsoft has added the BitLocker full-volume encryption feature that came out with Vista.

The Windows 7 version still uses a 128-bit or 256-bit AES encryption algorithm, but is now more flexible and simplifies drive encryption by automatically creating hidden boot partitions. The result, users no longer need to repartition their drives after installation. And where Vista users required a unique recovery key for each protected volume, Windows 7 users only need a single encryption key. A new feature called "BitLocker To Go" lets users encrypt removable storage devices with a password or a digital certificate.

New improvements for IT administrators

A plethora of new options that make life easier for IT professionals as shown below:

AppLocker

This new feature is a control policy that allows administrators to precisely spell out what applications users can run on their desktops. It can also be used to block unauthorized or unlicensed software and applications.

Multiple Active Firewall Policies

This feature provides a big improvement over Vista, which automatically set firewall policies depending on the type of network connection you chose such as home, public, or work. Remote Vista users couldn't connect to multiple networks while on the road, or if someone working from home used a VPN, he or she couldn't apply settings to connect to the corporate network. Windows 7's Multiple Active Firewall Policies allows IT professionals to create multiple sets of rules for remote and desktop employees.

DirectAccess

A feature provides a secure way to manage and update individual PCs remotely. It uses IPv6 and IPSec protocols to create a secure, two-way connection from a remote user's PC to the corporate network. Users benefit by not having to manually set up VPN connections and IT professionals enjoy the ease of distributing patches and updates whenever remote workers are connected to the network.

Improved Windows Search

Is a new feature which allows for faster more thorough searches, and also provides IT administrators with better per-user policy oversight and the ability to manage resource utilization by controlling how desktop search accesses network resources. Additional improvements were the seek-and-find capabilities with Federated Search, which combines desktop, SharePoint, and Internet search methods and allows users to scan external hard drives, networked PCs, and even remote data sources. Another new feature enables the user to search for identical copies of files on drives.

Upgraded Windows Recovery Environment

A feature Microsoft introduced in Vista and was a replacement of the Recovery Console in Windows XP. The new upgrade allows users to perform a range of system and data recovery functions, including checking for defective memory, repairing boot-level startup issues, returning the system to earlier configurations, and other features we will discuss later in this book.

AeroSnap Desktop Feature

This is a new feature of Windows desktop. If you pull a window to either edge of the desktop, it automatically makes each screen half the screen and compares the two windows side by side.

AeroPeek Desktop Feature

This is another new feature of Windows desktop. In XP and Vista you had a button to minimize all the windows and see the desktop. The problem was that all the windows you had minimized you then had to maximize one by one. The new button to the right of the clock makes all the windows invisible when pushed. You can even click on desktop items and open them. Press the button again and all your open windows come back the way they were before you pressed the button.

Improved Backup Utility

This improved backup utility now gives users control over which folders they want to back up which was a restriction in Vista, which allowed backups on a per-volume basis only.

Windows XP Mode and Windows Virtual PC

These two new features address issues of incompatibility for applications designed to run older XP applications. You will learn to configure this later in this book. This shows Microsoft is intent on retiring XP as a supported product in the near future.

Speed, lower resource utilization and invisible open windows

Most users of Windows 7 will tell you that this new operating system uses fewer resources which make it faster than its predecessor, Vista. While that ultimately will depend on each PC's RAM level and processor capabilities, Windows 7 does boot up and shut down faster that Vista or XP, in part because the new OS loads device drivers in parallel as opposed to serial.

In addition the Windows 7 user interface is also less cluttered and the Control Panel and shut down features are less confusing. And those annoying security pop ups? Windows 7 adds a slider feature that lets users decide if you want those or not. YAY! It reminds me of the MAC commercials where the secret service agent stands between the PC and the MAC guys and tries to intervene every time the PC tried to talk to the MAC and vice versa. MAC had a field day with those commercials.

The taskbar has been redesigned to resemble the Dock feature in Mac OS X. The new taskbar features a customizable lineup of program icons that users can click on to launch or switch between applications. But Microsoft did one better on Mac Dock; right-click on an application icon in the taskbar and you get a list of actions associated with it.

For example, the Microsoft Word icon will present a list of the most recently opened files, while Firefox will lay out a list of your most visited web sites.

Finally, Aero Peek is a new feature that can be activated by hovering your mouse over a small rectangle on the edge of the taskbar. Your windows all stay open but instantly become transparent revealing the icons and features of the desktop.

Minimum Hardware Requirements

The hardware requirements for Windows 7 are relatively close to those for Vista. This is an improvement. Speeds of processors and RAM have greatly increased since Vista was released where the requirements have virtually stayed the same. Windows 7 requirements:

- 1 GHz or faster 32-bit (x86) or a 64-bit (x64) processor
- 1GB RAM (32-bit)/2 GB RAM (64-bit)
- 16 GB available disk space (32-bit)/20 GB (64-bit)
- DirectX 9 graphics processor with WDDM 1.0 or higher driver.

Note: *Microsoft's free Windows 7 Upgrade Advisor can help you decide if your hardware will work; check it out at: www.Microsoft.com/windows/windows-7/get/upgrade-advisor.aspx.*

Driver and hardware support

Where this was an issue with CP driver not being compatible with Vista this does not seem to be an issue with Windows 7 which can use Vista drivers. There are some minor differences so Microsoft introduced the Application Compatibility Toolkit which allows IT professionals to inventory their applications and decide whether their applications are Windows 7-compatible. This way, companies can apply compatibility fixes if they are needed.

Windows 7 32-bit vs. 64-bit

Most people have no idea what upgrading to 64-bit gets you. You will see no upfront advantage if you are running 32-bit software on a 64-bit OS. You also lose the ability to run 16-bit software. If you have older DOS type application you should test to make sure it will work on and work properly on a 64-vit OS.

What you do get is more speed. More bits gets you access to more. The processor inside your PC communicates with your system memory (RAM). Thus, the maximum amount of memory a 32-bit processor can address is 4 gigabytes. 64-bit processors can address 17,179,869,184 gigabytes (16 exabytes) of RAM.

Most people will use Windows 7 64-bit to address the increasing demands for more RAM. But while 64-bit Windows 7 can run most 32-bit applications without a problem, it's not compatible with 32-bit hardware drivers or 32-bit utilities. This means you need a native 64-bit driver for every device on your PC which unless your PC and all your attached components have drivers to support 64-bit, finding support for all your hardware may be a bit of a challenge, especially on older computers.

The major benefit? 64-bit software running on 64-bit Windows 7 runs as much as 10% faster.

Now that we know all this, let's move on to Chapter 2 and learn about troubleshooitng Windows 7 software installations.

Chapter 2 - Software Installation and Troubleshooting

Software Installation Issues

Very few things aggravate your user base more than the inability to run one of their mission critical applications. As such it is tantamount we discuss software installation, compatibility, maintenance, and repair along with troubleshooting steps you can perform to resolve any issues you have during this process.

>**Note:** Working as an Enterprise Desktop Support Technician means that there is a 95% chance your workstations are joined to a domain, and have policies assigned to them. It is therefore vital that you are aware of the different policies in place, and how these policies would affect tasks such as software installation and maintenance.

Application deployment methods have become quite diversified! In an enterprise environment you may have applications running in XP Mode (explained in Chapter 3), RemoteApps running off of a server 2008 terminal server, locally installed, and web based applications all running on the same computer. Troubleshooting issues with these applications will vary depending which distribution method the application utilizes. We will discuss an overview of troubleshooting methods for each excluding XP mode troubleshooting, which will be addressed in Chapter 3.

Troubleshooting Locally Installed Software

Your first step in troubleshooting software installation issues is to verify that the software is compatible with Windows 7, and that all of the minimum requirements for running the software are met.

>**Note:** Before you spend hours trying to diagnose why a computer will not install an application, contact your network administrator and discuss what Software Restriction Policies and /or AppLocker rules are applied to the site, domain, and Organizational Unit the user and computer are stored in.

Once you have verified that the application is compatible with Windows 7, your machine meets all of the minimum system requirements, and none of the site, domain or Organizational Unit Policies would affect your software installation you will need to check the local machine's security policy to verify that no policies local to the computer are adversely affecting installation. The steps to do this are shown below.

1. Click on the Windows Orb (Start Button)
2. In the Search Bar type in secpol.msc and press enter
3. The local security policy window pops up as shown in Figure 2.1

4. Expand the Software Restriction Policies and Application Control Policies to verify that no local computer policies are preventing you from installing your application.

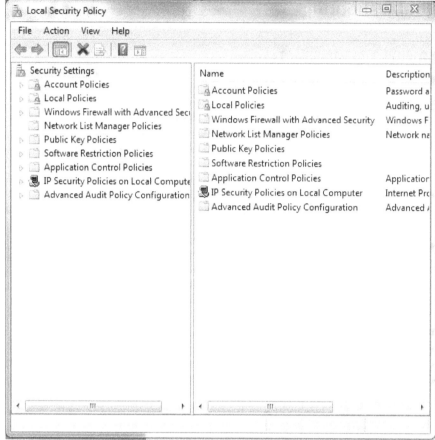

Figure 2.1

AppLocker

AppLocker as shown in Figure 2.2, it is a new application control feature available in Microsoft Windows 7 that helps eliminate unwanted and unknown applications within an organization's network providing a much more productive and secure environment.

AppLocker answers the need for application control with a simple and flexible application that allows administrators to specify exactly what is allowed to run on the computer in their network environment. There are many benefits to using AppLocker in your network such as:

- Stop unlicensed software from being installed or run in your environment.

- Preventing vulnerable, unauthorized applications from being installed or run in your environment.
- Prevent user from running applications which waste time.
- Stopping users from running applications that needlessly consume network bandwidth.
- Preventing users from running applications that possible contain viruses or malware.
- Allow users to install and run software and updates based upon their business needs
- Ensure compliance of corporate policies and industry regulations for PCI DSS, Sarbanes-Oxley, HIPAA, Basel II, and state identity theft protection acts.
- Reduce the cost of repair for users who install software which causes their PC to have issues or infects other devices in the network.

AppLocker provides a powerful solution using three rule types: allow, deny, and exception. Allow rules limit execution of applications to a "good list" of programs and applications. Deny rules take the opposite approach and disallow all programs and applications on the "bad list". Exception rules allow you to exclude files from an allow/deny rule that would normally be included such as a rule to "allow everything in the Windows Operating System to run, except the built-in games."

AppLocker is configured in the Group Policy Editor in Local Computer Policy, Security Settings, Application Control Policies, and then AppLocker as shown in Figure 2.2. In Figure 2.3 you will see the options that you can configure for AppLocker.

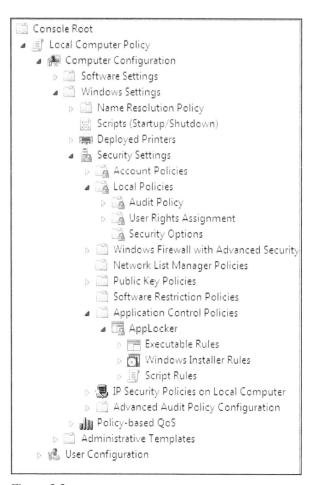

Figure 2.2

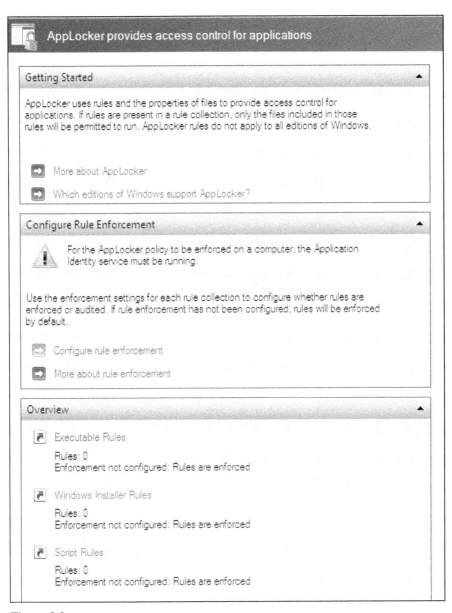

Figure 2.3

Troubleshooting with the System Configuration Applet (Msconfig)

The System Configuration Applet is a great utility that can be used to single out problem services or programs that are being loaded on boot. From personal experience I can attest to its effectiveness particularly with issues with a computer freezing immediately upon login and/or performing sluggishly on boot. A quick cleanup of your startup programs could save you minutes in total boot time! To get to the System Configuration Applet you will need to...

1. Click on the Windows Orb (Start Button)
2. Type in msconfig and hit Enter

Halving your troubleshooting Surface Area

Imagine you had a super computer with 1000 programs installed. Your boss tells you that one program is locking up the system immediately upon boot and wants to discover the culprit as quickly as possible. How would you go about finding this? How long would it take you? The answer might surprise you. If you went into the startup tab in the System Configuration Applet (Figure 2.4) and unchecked half of the programs on the list and rebooted, your troubleshooting surface area is reduced by 50%. If the issue is no longer present, you know that the issue resides in one the 500 startup items you eliminated, if it's still present then the program is still on the list of startup items. Depending on if the issue still present or not, you would either uncheck an additional 250 of the startup services left checked (if the issue is still present). Or uncheck all services and check 250 of the services left unchecked originally (if the issue was not present). This halving technique continues, and in 8 reboots you have your answer.

As you can see from Figure 2.4 other system configuration tabs are available for you later in this book.

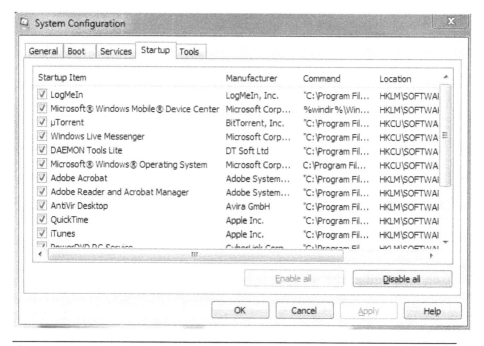

Figure 2.4

Software Installation Permissions

Depending on the software you are installing you might have to install the software as a local Administrator. It also would be a good idea to verify the user has write permissions to the directories that the application is attempting to install to. If you try to install an application that requires Administrator permissions and rights, a UAC (User Account Control) dialog box will pop-up asking you to enter in the credentials of a local Administrator.

Logs are an IT professional's best friend

As an IT Professional, I am inundated with calls from users who want help troubleshooting a problem with their application. After hearing a detailed account of their issue, one of the firsts troubleshooting tasks I perform is to check the application and system logs for clues as to what the problem might be. To do this you will need to...

1. Click on the Windows Orb (Start Button).
2. Right-Click Computer and Click Manage
3. Expand Event Viewer
4. Expand Windows Logs

You will then have 5 logs available for you to view, Application, Security, Setup, System, and Forwarded Events.

- Application: This log holds information, warnings, errors, and critical events related to the applications you have running on your computer.

- Security: This log is used to create an audit trail of user logon, permission, privilege use, object access, and the success or failure of those audits depending on your audit policy.

- Setup: Used on Domain Controllers, can be safely ignored

- System: This log holds information, warnings, errors, and critical events pertaining to Windows and Windows Services.

- Forwarded Events: Used to store Events forwarded to your computer from other computers.

Using the Application and System Logs

When troubleshooting an application problem you will want to look at both the application and the system logs to help you determine the cause of the issue. Once you have found warnings, errors, or critical events that you believe merit further investigation, and that could be related to the problem you are experiencing try looking up the events online; chances are someone else has experienced the exact same issue and a resolution has been documented.

Filtering out verbose and Informational events

Wouldn't it be nice if you could instantly view all of the warnings, errors, or critical errors found within a log without having to scroll through thousands of verbose or informational log entries or wait for the computer to sort the logs by category? This is actually quite easy to do and is outlined below.

1. In Computer Management, Expand Event Viewer and click on the log you want to view.

2. In the Actions pane on the right hand side of the log click on Filter Current Log.

3. You are presented with a variety of filter options as shown in Figure 12.5, check the Critical, Warning, and Error check boxes in the event level category and click ok.

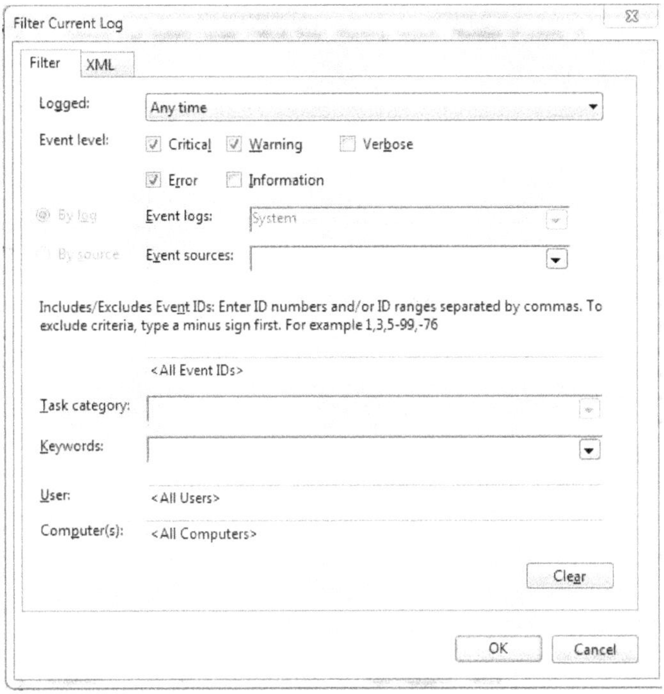

Filter Current Log

Filter | XML

Logged: Any time

Event level: ☑ Critical ☑ Warning ☐ Verbose

☑ Error ☐ Information

◉ By log   Event logs: System

☐ By source   Event sources:

Includes/Excludes Event IDs: Enter ID numbers and/or ID ranges separated by commas. To exclude criteria, type a minus sign first. For example 1,3,5-99,-76

<All Event IDs>

Task category:

Keywords:

User: <All Users>

Computer(s): <All Computers>

Clear

OK   Cancel

Figure 2.5

Recently Added Programs

Although Windows has built-in resource management systems that prevent applications from using resources allocated to another application, there are still errors that can occur due to applications interacting with each other. If a user suddenly reports a problem with an application, in addition to checking the Event Viewer for clues as to the underlying cause, it would also be a good idea to check the Programs and Features applet of the control panel to see what has recently been installed. The steps to do this are outlined below.

1. Click on the Windows Orb (Start Button)
2. Click on Control Panel
3. Click on Programs
4. Once you are in the programs section, click on Programs and Features.
5. You are presented with a list of programs that are currently installed on your local machine as shown in Figure 2.6. Click the Installed On tab to organize this list by installation date.

Uninstall or change a program

To uninstall a program, select it from the list and then click Uninstall, Change, or Repair.

Organize ▾

Name	Publisher	Installed On	Size
Starcraft		11/24/2009	
LogMeIn	LogMeIn, Inc.	11/23/2009	38.5 MB
7-Zip 4.65 (x64 edition)	Igor Pavlov	11/23/2009	3.98 MB
Magic ISO Maker v5.4 (build 0239)		11/23/2009	
Microsoft Office Enterprise 2007		11/22/2009	
Microsoft SQL Server 2005 Compact Edition [ENU]	Microsoft Corporation	11/21/2009	1.72 MB
Bonjour	Apple Inc.	11/21/2009	609 KB
iTunes	Apple Inc.	11/21/2009	133 MB
NVIDIA PhysX	NVIDIA Corporation	11/21/2009	120 MB
Adobe Reader 9.2	Adobe Systems Incorporated	11/21/2009	208 MB
Apple Mobile Device Support	Apple Inc.	11/21/2009	40.8 MB
Microsoft Visual C++ 2008 Redistributable - x86 9.0.3...	Microsoft Corporation	11/21/2009	596 KB
Microsoft Silverlight	Microsoft Corporation	11/21/2009	14.9 MB
Windows Live Sync	Microsoft Corporation	11/21/2009	2.78 MB

Figure 2.6

Repairing / Modifying / Uninstalling a program

The Programs and Features applet can also be used to uninstall / change / or repair an installed application (assuming your application supports these actions). Simply select the application from the list and all possible actions associated with the installed application are listed above.

Licensing

Depending on what software you are installing, licensing restrictions may prevent you from installing an application. Verify that you are not out of licenses for the software before installing, or if the program will not activate.

Problem Steps Recorder

The problem Steps Recorder as shown in Figures 2.7, 2.8 and 2.9, is an awesome new feature included in Windows 7 that lets users record the problem they are experiencing, as well as highlight problem areas and provide detailed comments explaining the issue. It works by taking a series of screenshots anytime an object is clicked. Once the recording session is done, the user is prompted to save the file as zip. You then have the user send you the zip file, unzip and open the file in internet explorer as the file format is MHTML. The MHTML file contains the screenshots of taken, comments made by the user, user interaction with the application, a timestamp of when the recording placed, and information regarding the program and OS versions. The following screenshots from a sample recording.

Problem Step 2: (1/12/2010 8:11:51 PM) User Comment "I need a cd???"

Return to top of page...

Additional Details

The following section contains the additional details that were recorded that can help find a solution for your problem.
These details help accurately identify the programs and UI you used while recording the problem steps.
This section may contain text that is internal to programs that only very advanced users or programmers may understand.
Please review these details to ensure that they do not contain any information that you would not like others to see

on: 1/12/2010 8:11:33 PM - 8:11:53 PM

3, Missed Steps: 0, Other Errors: 0

n: 7600.16385.amd64fre.win7_rtm.090713-1255 6.1.0.0.2.1

User left double click on "Starcraft - Brood War (list item)" in "Program Manager"
: Explorer, 6.1.7600.16385 (win7_rtm.090713-1255), Microsoft Corporation, EXPLORER.EXE, EXPLOI
ircraft - Brood War, Desktop, FolderView, SysListView32, SHELLDLL_DefView, Program Manager, P:

User Comment: "I need a cd???"

Figure 2.7

69

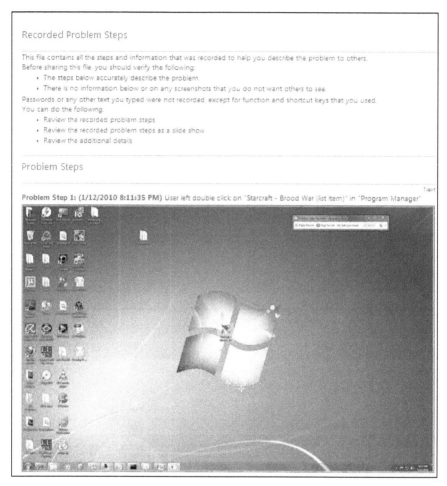

Figure 2.8

To open the problem steps recorder do the following:

1. Click on the Windows ORB (Start Button)
2. In the Search Bar type in PSR.exe and press enter.

As you can see from Figure the interface is minimalistic but quite affective.

Figure 2.9

System Restore

Although System Restore has been around since XP, it has been given a nice new feature in Windows 7 that lets you determine what programs and drivers will be removed if the restore is performed. To perform a system restore simply...

1. Click the Windows Orb (Start Button)
2. In the Search Bar type in System Restore and press enter.

   OR

1. Click the Windows Orb (Start Button)
2. Click on Control Panel
3. Click System and Security
4. Click on Backup and Restore
5. Click on the option to Recover System Settings or your Computer
6. Click Open System Restore

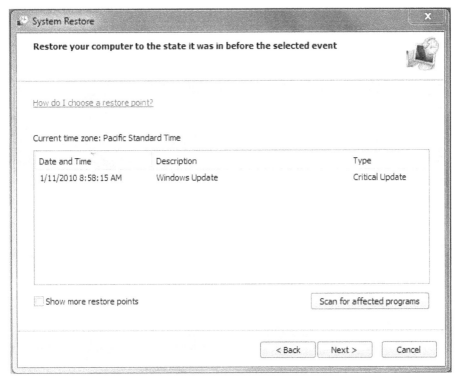

Figure 2.10

As you can see from Figure 2.10 and 2.11, in terms of the user interface not much has changed. By default, only the most recent restore point is available for restore, but if you click show more restore points all possible restore points are shown starting with the most recent.

The scan for affected programs button scans your computer to determine what programs and/or drivers will be removed if you choose the selected restore point and then displays the results in a window shown in Figure.

This feature is a great way to determine what system restore point you will need to use to remove a program or driver that is causing issues. Once you have chosen the restore point you'd like to use, click next. You are warned that if you have changed your password recently it is advisable you create a password reset disk. Do so if needed and click finish to perform the restore.

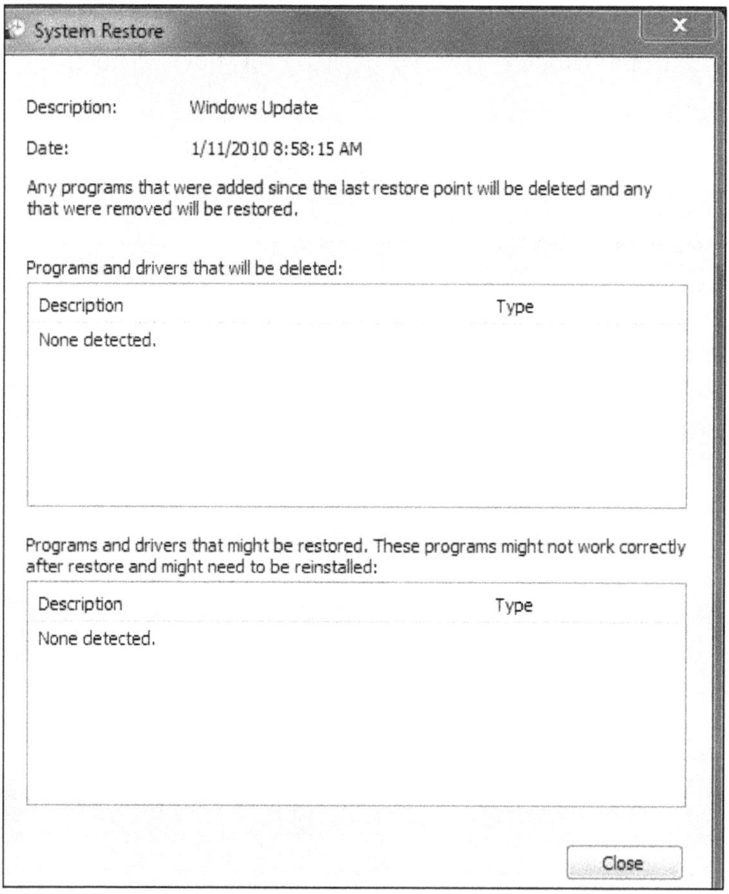

Figure 2.11

Troubleshooting Web Applications

Web applications use a variety of programming languages that work in the background to deliver the vivid pages we crave. Although the majority of the time these pages are seamlessly handled by your browser, from time to time issues can arise. Troubleshooting web applications is easier than troubleshooting locally installed applications, because the problems are browser centric versus system wide. Many problems can be fixed simply by verifying all ActiveX controls for the website are installed, your browser is up to date, and the latest version of the most common web technologies are installed (EX: Adobe Flash, Shockwave, Reader, and Sun Microsystems Java).

Internet Explorer ActiveX and Group Policy

Like the majority of Windows, settings in Group Policy can granularly control every aspect of internet explorer including the installation of ActiveX controls in addition to locking down what websites the user can visit. Again, as discussed previously you will need to contact your network administrator and verify no Site, Domain, or Organizational Unit GPO's could potentially be causing the issue. Once this has been verified you will need to determine if any locally instituted GPO's are causing the issue. Follow the steps outlined below to perform this task.

    1. Click on the Windows Orb (Start Button)

    2. In the Search Bar type in GPEDIT.msc and press enter

    3. Internet Explorer Group Policy settings are controlled in both the User and Computer sections of Group Policy so you will need to expand the Administrative Templates\Windows Components\Internet Explorer settings of both sections to determine if any settings are adversely affecting Internet Explorer.

ActiveX Installer Service (AXIS)

Until the release of Windows Vista, it was difficult for Administrators to mitigate the threat of ActiveX controls installed via Internet Explorer. In addition, ActiveX installers require you to be logged on as a local Administrator. For enterprise environments that have policies dictating the majority of users not have a local Administrator account this can severely hamper workplace efficiency as users have to call the help desk just to get an ActiveX control installed. The ActiveX installer service first seen in Windows Vista addresses these issues by allowing administrators to specify which sites standard users can install ActiveX controls on. Unlike Vista however ActiveX installer service is enabled by default. Settings are controlled through Group Policy on the Site, Domain, Organizational Unit, and Local Level. Determination of local ActiveX Group Policies is done using the following steps:

    1. Click on the Windows Orb (Start Button)

    2. In the Search Bar type in GPEDIT.msc and press enter

3. Expand Computer Configuration\Administrative Template\Windows Components

4. Click on ActiveX installer service

The policy object has two settings for you edit, Approved Installation Sites for ActiveX Controls, and ActiveX installation policy for sites in Trusted zones, like all GPO settings a detailed description of the options associated with the setting are given as illustrated in Figure 2.12.

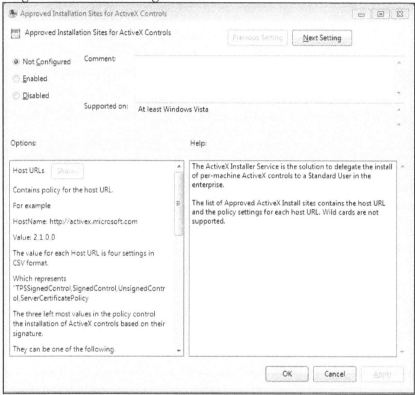

Figure 2.12

> **Note:** Be aware that in both the computer and user configuration sections of the local Group policy in the Administrative Templates\Windows Components\Internet Explorer\Security Features\Restrict ActiveX Install Section, you can specify that you don't want to allow internet explorer and/or any Windows process to install any ActiveX controls.

Internet Explorer Add-Ons

Add-ons to Internet Explorer can conflict with existing Add-ons causing all sorts of unwanted behavior. If you suspect a recently installed Add-on is causing errors with your Web Applications you will need to manage the Add-ons by performing the following actions...

1. Open up Internet Explorer
2. Click on Tools > Internet Options
3. Click the Programs tab and Click Manage add-ons

You are given a list of currently loaded add-ons, their publisher, status, and versions as well as the option to show all installed add-ons as show in Figure 2.13. From here you can disable add-ons as well as discover the version of the add-ons you are using. Unfortunately, there is no installed on tab to determine if any add-ons were recently installed.

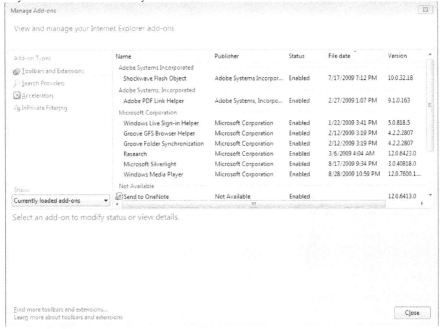

Figure 2.13

Additional Web Application Troubleshooting Steps

If a websites ActiveX control seems to be corrupted, try uninstalling the program associated with the ActiveX control by using the Programs and Features section of the Control Panel. Then reinstall the ActiveX control from the website you originally installed it from.

If the problem seems to be Internet Explorer specific, first try running the website with compatibility view enabled. You can do this by clicking on the broken page icon in the address bar. If this does not fix your issue, try running an alternate browser such as Firefox or Opera and see if the problem is still present.

Troubleshooting RemoteApps

As a Desktop Support Technician, most issues with RemoteApps are beyond your control. In reality a RemoteApps is simply a terminal services session modified to only show the remotely running application. If a user is having issues with a Remote App a first step would be to log off the users terminal services session and have them reopen the remote app.

If many users report having issues running RemoteApps you should discuss with your Network Administrator the problems experienced and consider repackaging your RemoteApps deployment. Since RemoteApps use terminal services as the underlying technology you will need to make sure the clipboard, printers, and drives are available in the terminal services session so that the end user can copy and paste into the RemoteApp, print to a local printer, and access information stored on locally connected drives.

> **Note:** The goal of a RemoteApps is create an overall user experience that behaves like the program is installed locally. That being said one give away is shown in Figure in which when you click on My Computer in a RemoteApp, you will be given the option to connect to the drives on your local machine as shown in Figure 2.14. Otherwise if you are unsure if the installation is local or remote, check Programs and Features in Control Panel to see if the program is listed.

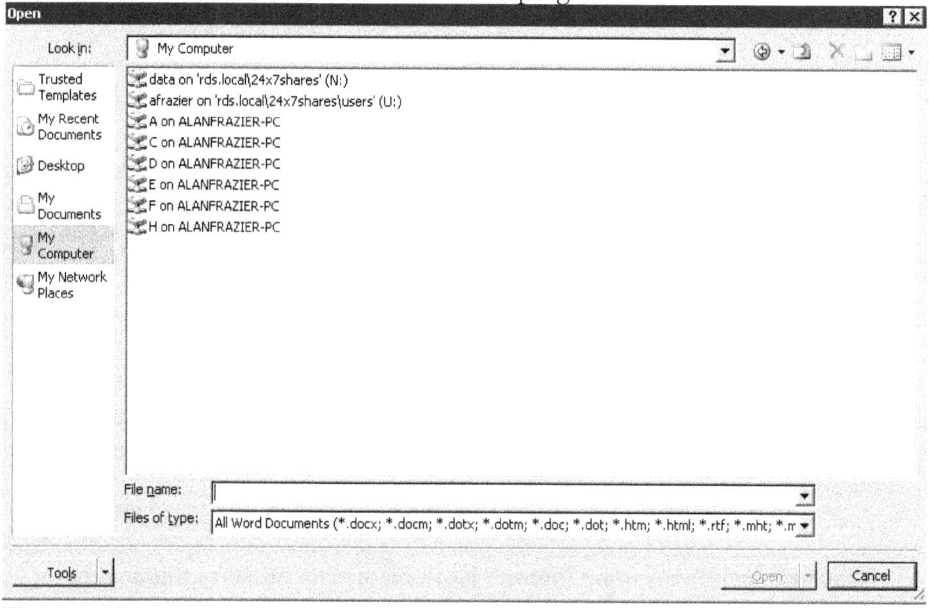

Figure 2.14

Additional Software Troubleshooting Tips

Workstation Images

Most enterprise environments use images as an efficient basis for implementing large scale computer deployments, or should a workstation have an issue a baseline image can quickly and easily be restored. Keep in mind however, that depending on your software licensing structure, you may need to remove any licenses from a baseline image, before deploying the image to your workstations. This is usually done by removing specific keys from the registry. Be sure to verify all software on the baseline machine runs and all features function correctly. This is critical as any mistakes made on the baseline machine will have to be fixed on all machines subsequently imaged.

Software issues caused by hardware failure

An array of software issues can result from a PC having a hardware failure. Two of the most common hardware failures are a bad hard drive or bad RAM. If either of these components have issues they can result in numerous problems in the operating system including but not limited to problems with software. If you suspect hardware failure may be the culprit, check the system log in event viewer for problems such as NTFS corruption, Page Faults, Hard Drive Controller errors, Bad Blocks, and messages indicating unexpected reboots. In my early years as a computer technician I would often spend hours trying to solve an issue in the operating system only to discover that a hardware component had failed.

Programs Interacting with Network Resources

If a program is stored, or has data stored on a network resource, problems can occur if the network resource becomes unavailable. If your user complains that a program is not functioning correctly, or is prompting for a path to a data folder, and network documentation shows that the application uses a network share or resource, one of the first troubleshooting steps you should perform is to verify the user has access to the network and its resources. If a program uses a specific network share, create a mapped network drive on the user's computer for that share to verify network and resource connectivity and user access permissions. If a mapped network drive is already used verify the network drive is not disconnected.

Programs that use specific hardware

If a program that interfaces with a specific hardware device such as a scanner, printer, or proprietary component is giving you issues as it interacts with the device the culprit may not be the program, but the device itself. Additionally you could be using an outdated driver, or the firmware loaded on the device

---

could need to be upgraded. To update the driver or firmware of the device, consult the device manufactures online resources.

The devil is in the details

When troubleshooting software issues it is imperative that you collect as much background information as possible before you attempt any resolution. First, deduce the scale of the problem. Is it isolated to a particular user, group, or network segment? If the issue is happening to many users simultaneously the cause is most likely a server or network component which you may or may not be responsible for. If the issue is isolated, the cause is most likely local to their machine. Once you have determined that the problem is affecting only a specific user or computer, have the affected user(s) explain in detail what the problem is, the frequency in which it occurs, and steps they have already taken in attempts to resolve the issue.

Additional Questions to Ask

Additional questions you might ask include, how long has this issue been present? Have there been any recent changes to the affected system? To your knowledge have you been experiencing any symptoms that may indicate the presence of malware? Have experienced any other problems recently? Learning how to ask the right questions can save you countless hours and keep your user base happy as you efficiently resolve any issue they encounter.

Chapter 3 – Software Compatibility-XP Mode(XPM)

An enterprise environment often has unique, mission critical, large scale software installations that are updated very infrequently if at all. The cost to migrate away from these installations is so prohibitive that you may be asked to innovatively tweak these legacy applications to run on the most modern hardware and software.

When Windows Vista came out in 2007 it took a while for application makers to make their programs 100% compatible with Windows Vista, and as such many people decided to stick with XP until their favorite application was updated.

Vista like XP had a compatibility tab (reviewed later in this chapter) that let you change the way the application was run on the computer in the hopes that it would allow the application to run successfully. If that didn't work however you then had to search various internet forums for workarounds (which may or may not violate your license agreement with the developer by modifying the application) and/or check the software developer's website for patches and updates that would address the issue. If you were one of the unlucky tech's that was responsible for a mission critical application that had no workarounds available and was written by a lazy software developer that had no imminent or foreseeable plans of updating their code you were in effect doomed to stick with your legacy operating system or create virtual machines running the compatible operating system for your users to use. Windows 7 adds another tool to your compatibility arsenal that works on top of Virtual PC to address this ongoing problem. Please welcome to the stage Windows XP Mode.

XP Mode Requirements

- Windows 7 Professional, Ultimate or Enterprise

- At least 2 GB of RAM

- A processor that supports Hardware Virtualization

- Hardware Virtualization Enabled in the BIOS

What windows XP Mode can do for you

As a enterprise support technician it should be your endeavor (to ensure your continued employment) to identify ways for your company to cut costs when it comes to their IT infrastructure without sacrificing any of their existing application installations or the overall performance and user experience of the network. Windows XP Mode helps you meet those goals in that it is freely available from Microsoft as a download and comes with a preconfigured fully licensed copy of XP service pack 3 available for you to use to run your legacy applications. This means that you don't have to worry about violating your licensing agreements with Microsoft or allocating time to prepare an XP machine be it either virtual or physical for use by end users to run their older applications.

XP Mode and them darn 16 bit apps

A fact that you have to be aware of as you decide whether or not to deploy 64 or 32 bit versions of Windows 7 on your client computers is that 16 bit applications will not run on a 64 bit operating system. This means that if you have ancient applications that were written for a 16 bit operating system you have to run this application in a 16 or 32 bit environment. Windows XP Mode resolves this issue by running in 32 bit.

Benefits of XP Mode

One of the key benefits (other than XP Mode not requiring a license) of running your legacy applications in XP Mode is that they are available in both the start menu of your XP mode virtual PC as well as your host Windows 7 operating system. A shortcut is created in the start menu of Windows 7 named Windows XP Mode Applications that lets users quickly click on an application that is installed in XP mode. The application is automatically opened up and runs like any other application installed on the computer except for the fact that it doesn't have transparent borders and the icon on the taskbar for the program is Virtual PC. This creates a very fluid experience for your end users.

Limitations of XP Mode

XP Mode will not efficiently run graphically intensive applications or applications that rely on special hardware equipment due to its virtualization properties.

Getting Started with XP Mode

Your first step in installing XP Mode is going online and downloading the XP Mode setup file as well as virtual PC. Microsoft's website makes it a very easy task as show in Figure 3.1, just choose your Windows 7 version and follow the step-by-step guide.

Link to download XP Mode:

http://www.microsoft.com/windows/virtual-pc/download.aspx

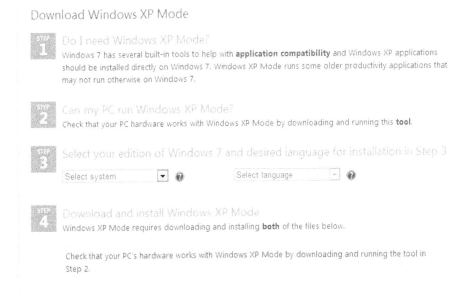

Figure 3.1

Once you have XP Mode and Virtual PC installed you will be prompted to reboot. After rebooting you can then access XP Mode by simply typing XP Mode into the search bar.

The XP Mode Setup Process

The first time you start XP Mode, you will be taken to a setup wizard to configure your installation. Accept the EULA and click next. Choose an installation Folder and password as shown in Figure 1.2. This password will be used to login to the default user in XP Mode XPMUser, however if you click remember credentials, the default user is automatically logged in. Choose your installation folder and credential options and click next.

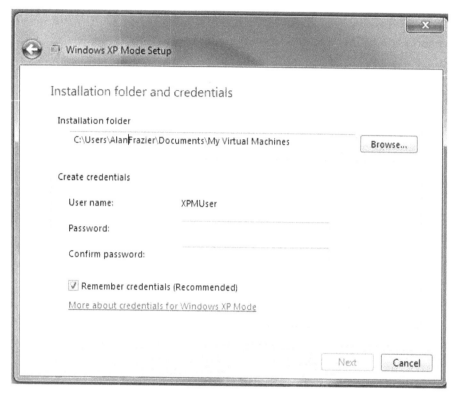

Figure 3.3

You are then prompted to turn on automatic updates as shown in Figure 3.3. Your only options are to turn it on or wait till later.

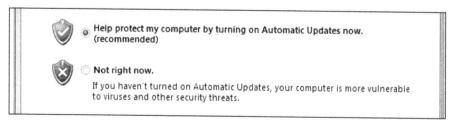

Figure 3.3

In the next window you are warned that by default setup shares your drives with XP Mode for ease of use, but this can be a security hole if you aren't careful about what you install (Figure 3.4).

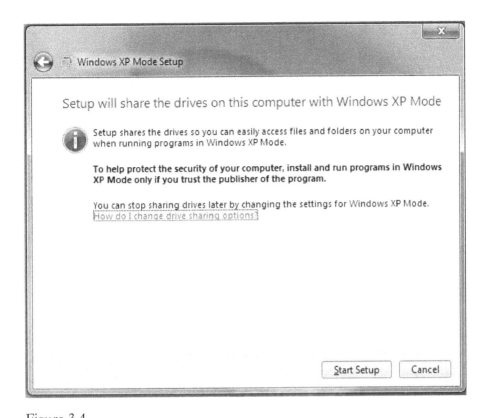

Figure 3.4

Click on Start Setup and Windows does the rest.

> **Alert:** XP Mode shares folders, and has the capability of sharing a USB flash device with your Host Operating System. This poses a security risk. To reduce this risk, be sure to install an antivirus solution on both Windows 7 and your XP Mode virtual machine in addition to regularly performing Windows updates.

Troubleshooting Problems with XP Mode

If you have installed an application in XP Mode and the shortcut to the application is not showing up in Windows XP Mode Applications in Windows 7, Boot XP Mode, and try copying the shortcut to the application into the start menu directory within the all users profile. Also, be aware XP Mode has a list of programs that it will not create a shortcut for in Windows 7 due to compatibility issues. The exclusion list can be found and modified in the registry by performing the followings steps...

1. Boot Windows XP Mode and Login

2. Click on Start > Click Run, type regedit and press enter.

3. Navigate to the following registry key

   HKEY_LOCAL_MACHINE\SOFTWARE\Microsoft\Windows NT\CurrentVersion\Virtual Machine\VPCVAppExcludeList

4. Delete the registry entry of the program you'd like to show up in the XP Mode Applications folder in Windows 7 and restart XP Mode.

Because XP Mode is merely a modified virtual machine, the same troubleshooting steps you use to diagnose and repair issues with an XP workstation can be used with XP Mode. The exception being that because the machine is virtual, the chances of you experiencing blue screens caused by driver issues are slim to none.

If you start experiencing unstable XP Mode Applications or frequent XP Mode blue Screens, verify the integrity of the hardware of your Windows 7 Host Operating System in addition to checking your event logs for errors and warnings. Also, it would be advisable to run check disk on your boot partition in addition to the partition where the XP Mode directory was created in Windows 7 to clean up any file system corruption.

Compatibility Tab

Just about every executable file on your computer has a compatibility tab. All of the options listed, can be chosen automatically for you by running the Program Compatibility troubleshooter (discussed later in this chapter), but sometimes it's faster to manually select your compatibility options.

To access the compatibility tab you will need to...

1. Right-Click the exe file of the program you are experiencing an issue with.

2. Choose properties

3. Click on the compatibility tab.

Your options are enumerated in Figure 3.5.

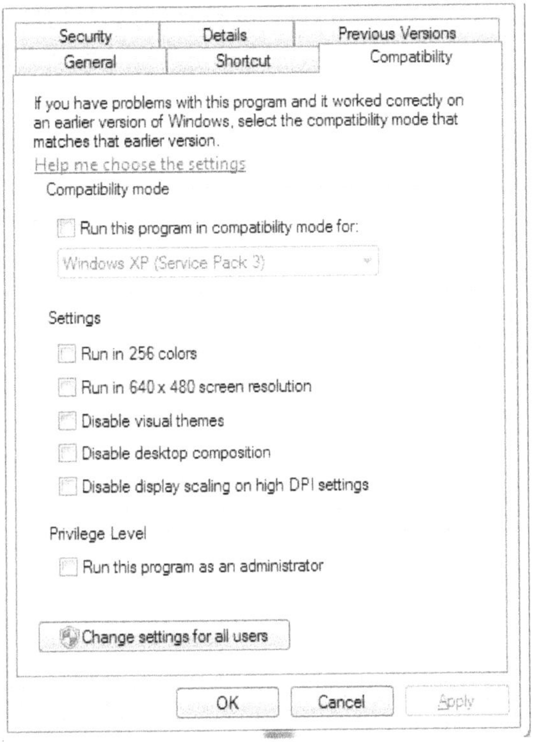

| Security | Details | Previous Versions |
| General | Shortcut | Compatibility |

If you have problems with this program and it worked correctly on an earlier version of Windows, select the compatibility mode that matches that earlier version.

Help me choose the settings

Compatibility mode

☐ Run this program in compatibility mode for:

Windows XP (Service Pack 3)

Settings

☐ Run in 256 colors

☐ Run in 640 x 480 screen resolution

☐ Disable visual themes

☐ Disable desktop composition

☐ Disable display scaling on high DPI settings

Privilege Level

☐ Run this program as an administrator

🛡 Change settings for all users

| OK | Cancel | Apply |

Figure 3.5

Programs Section of the Troubleshooting Applet

The Program Compatibility Troubleshooter is one of the many troubleshooters listed in Troubleshooting applet of the Control Panel automates the process of selecting options found in the compatibility tab of your programs main executable file. First you select the program from a list of detected programs, or choose "Not listed" to browse your computer for the program files location (Figure 3.6).

Once you have selected the program or program file location you will then be given the option to choose whether you want to try the recommended settings or troubleshoot the program.

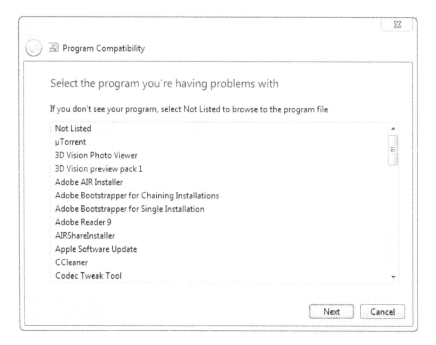

Figure 3.6

If you choose to try the recommended settings Windows makes a best guess as to what settings the program will be compatible with and then gives you a button to start the program. When it detects you have clicked the start the program button you then can click next again and are given a screen stating that the troubleshooter has completed and is the problem fixed? You have a choice between 3 options.

1. Yes, save these settings for this program

2. No, try again using different settings

3. No, report the problem to Microsoft and check for a solution online.

No, try again using different settings brings you to the same screen you would have been brought to had you clicked on the, "Troubleshoot the Program" button at the beginning of the troubleshooter. You are asked what problems do you notice and are given a series of checkboxes for you to describe what's going wrong. (Figure 3.7)

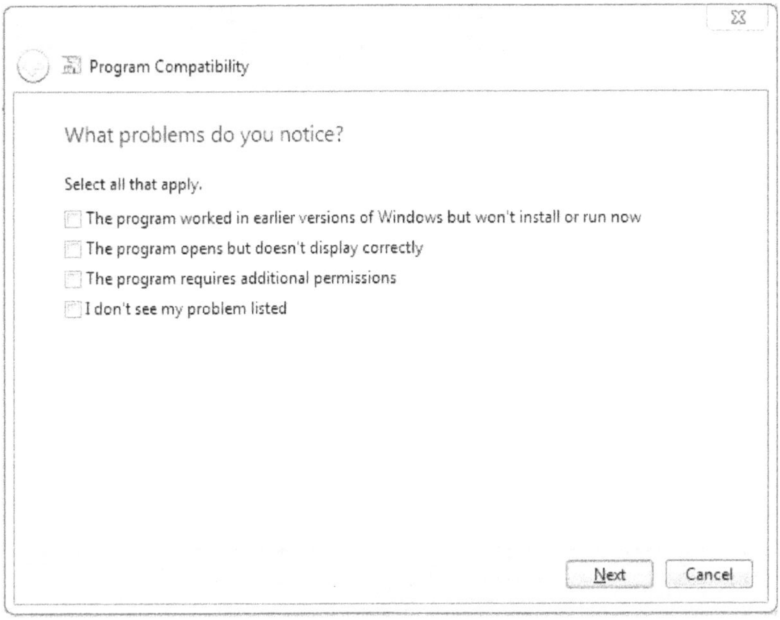

Figure 3.7

Depending on the options that you check Windows will ask you additional questions such as what operating system the program originally ran on and/or what display problems you are experiencing. If you choose I don't know when what Operating System the program was originally run on, Windows XP (Service Pack 2) is chosen by default.

Once the questions have been answered regarding the problems you are having with the program, you are then brought to the screen asking you to start the program. After you have tried to start the program click on next and you are brought to the troubleshooter has completed screen with the 3 options discussed earlier.

Chapter 4 Control Panel – User Accounts and Profiles

Windows 7 is the most secure version of Windows, Microsoft has ever developed.
Included in Windows 7 are some very good options for keeping your account secure. From passwords, to times your kids or workers can log in to Windows, all the way to the rating types of games and movies they can watch. This is all in an effort to keep your family as secure as possible.

In this chapter, you'll learn how to set up multiple users on a PC, select the right account type for different users, join a domain, enable Parental Controls, and much more.

We will also look at how to share your printers, hard disks and devices on the network. Then we will walk through the options you need to know to configure your Windows 7 personalized experience.

Configuring a User Account with Parental Controls

Under the Control Panel, User Accounts and Family Safety as shown in Figure 4.1, you have the options to add, modify, or delete user or administrator accounts. There are also many other items from parental controls to controlling what applications can be run. In this section we will cover all of them.

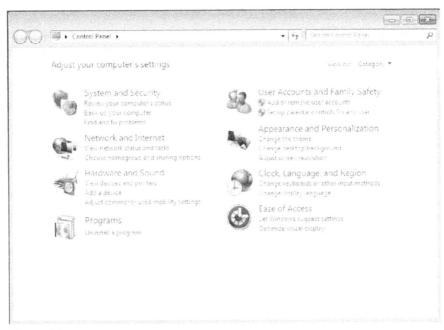

Figure 4.1

I quickly added another account and made it a user account called, "My Kids" as shown in Figure 4.2. After the account is created you can use this screen to change the account name, password, picture, or the account type. You can also setup the Parental Controls or delete the account.

Figure 4.2

I am going to click on Parental Controls as shown in Figure 4.2. When I do this it gives me the option to choose the user to modify as shown in Figure 4.3.

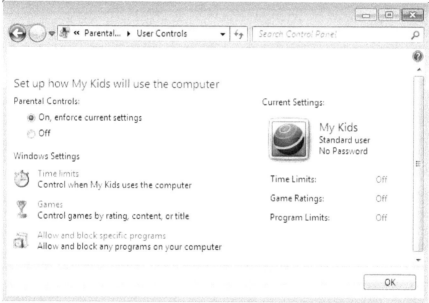

Figure 4.3

You will notice in Figure 4.3, under the picture that there are no Parental Controls configured. Next, I want to keep my kids off the computer after 8PM at night and not let them use it until 7AM. So I will click on Time Limits and use my mouse to highlight the times I want to keep the kids from logging in as shown in Figure 4.4.

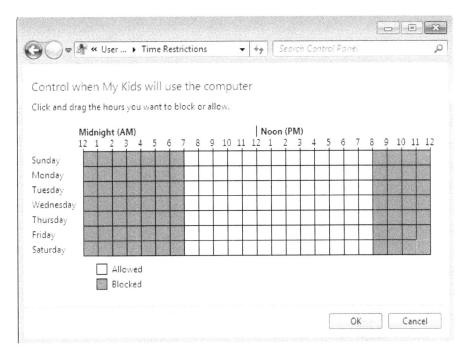

Figure 4.4

Now, there are definitely lots of games I would never let me kids see. In Figure 4.5 I set the maturity level for games and movies played under the My Kids login to Everyone 10+. This means that all the games with a Teen, Mature, or Adult content will be blocked.

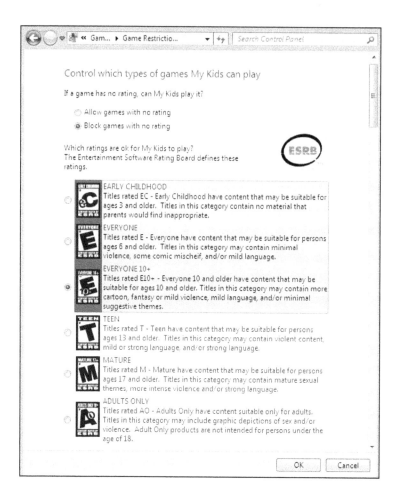

Figure 4.5

In Figure 4.6 you see the Parental Controls which allow you to keep your kids from using any program or application installed on the PC. Any application that is not checked cannot be used by the user logged in as My Kids.

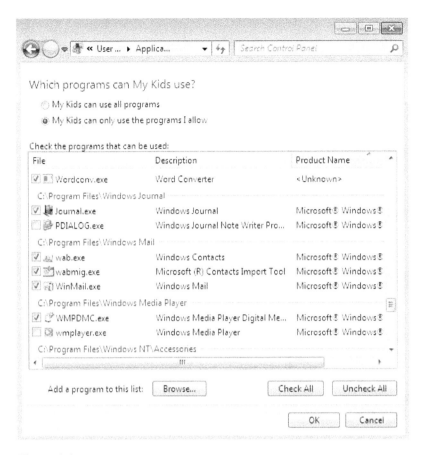

Figure 4.6

In the last screenshot in this section we will go back and review the changes we have made to the user My Kids as shown in Figure 4.7

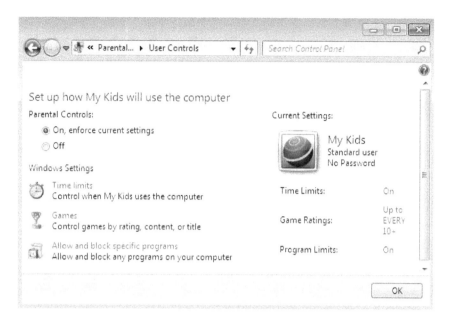

Figure 4.7

Advanced Sharing Settings

Windows 7 doesn't allow your printers or data to be shared by default. In fact it doesn't even let your PC be discovered on the network. These are all options you have to turn on yourself. In Figure 4.8, you see the Control Panel, Network and Sharing, Advanced sharing settings window. This is where you configure the options to share your printers, data, or allow other computers to see your computer on the network.

Figure 4.8

You will notice in Figure 4.8 that you have the ability to turn on or off the ability to be discovered on the network, turn on or off file and print sharing, and turn on or off the folders you want to publically share.

Linking Your Online ID's

Microsoft allows you to link your online ID's from websites like Live so that you can get online content without the need to continuously log in to the sites. In Figure 4.9, you see the Link Online ID's window found under the Control Panel, User Accounts and Family Safety, User Accounts. The link is on the left pane.

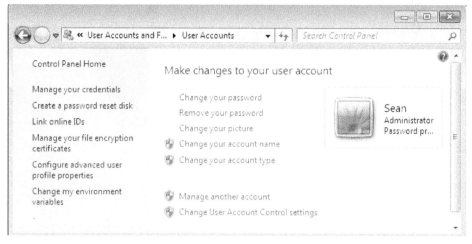

Figure 4.9

After you select Link online ID's you will see a list of the possible users that you can link ID's for. If there is only one account as I have configured you will immediately get the screen as shown in Figure 4.10. Notice the Windows Live icon allowing you to link your Windows Live ID.

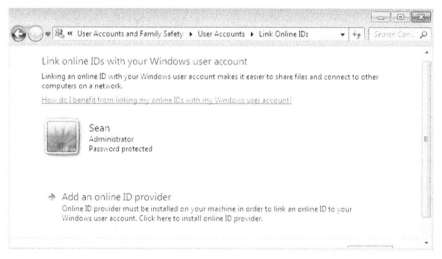

Figure 4.10

You will immediately be redirected to the Internet to sign in and allow your Windows Live ID as shown in Figure 4.11. We were given a rereleased copy of Windows 7 Enterprise which only has Windows Live as options. Microsoft however intends to add Bing, MSN and other logins as well.

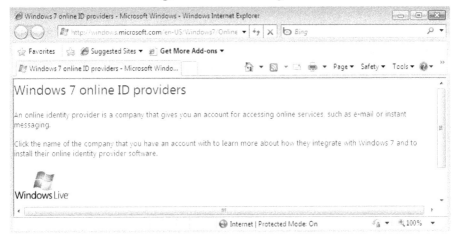

Figure 4.11

Joining a Domain

If you belong to a company, most likely you will be joining a domain. Where you configure this is kind of hidden if you are used to Windows XP and or previous versions.

Under System and Security in the Control Panel you will find the System link. Click on that and you will see the screen below in Figure 4.12. Notice I am currently in a Workgroup.

Figure 4.12

But in order to get all the benefits of a domain we have to join an Active Directory Domain. First click on Change settings and the screen in Figure 4.13 will appear. Now this looks similar to the one in Windows XP.

Figure 4.13

It gives us the computer name and then Workgroup we are in. Next let's click on Change and we will get the screen shown in Figure 4.14.

Figure 4.14

When you have entered your domain name and clicked on the Domain radio button you will get a popup which requires a member of the Domain Admins group to enter their credentials to join as shown in Figure 4.15.

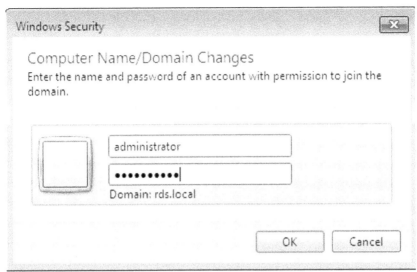

Figure 4.15

You will then get a popup the says "Welcome to the <Your Domain>." as shown in Figure 4.16.

Figure 4.16

Normally in a Windows book it would stop here and tell you to do a reboot. But this is not a certification book, it is a real world guide and before I reboot I go one step further to save me a lot of time.

If you rebooted, the only person who could install applications or make system changes is anyone in the Domain Admins group. I like to save myself time and add the user of this PC to the Power Users.

If you don't add it before you reboot from adding the PC to the domain, you have to login as an administrator and give the user Power User or

Administrator group rights, then log back out and log back in as the user to install applications.

I am the administrator and this is my laptop, so I am going to add myself to the Administrators group on the local PC. To do this, right click on the My Computer icon in the Start Bar. Choose Manage and you will get the Computer Management screen as shown in Figure 4.17.

Click on the Local Users and Groups, then choose Groups, Administrators (Or Power Users) and enter the login ID of the person you want to give the rights to. Now this will not give the person any extra domain rights but it will allow the user control over their own PC.

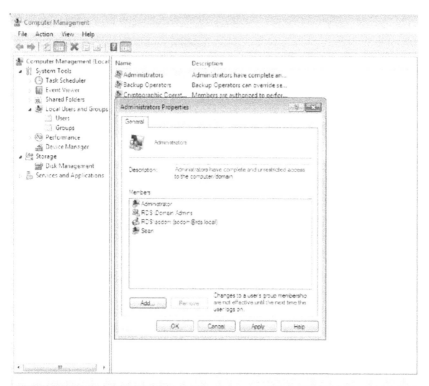

Figure 4.17

You will probably need the domain administrator's login and password one more time to add a domain user to any of the groups. Click Ok, find the restart screen from when you added the PC to the domain and click OK again as shown in Figure 4.18.

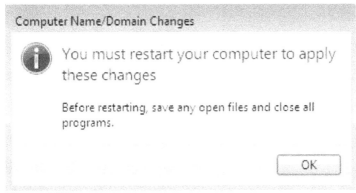

Figure 4.18

Personalization

We will look at personalizing your Windows 7 experience in this chapter. As you can see, you can make changes in the Control Panel, Appearance and Personalization then choose Personalization in Figure 4.19.

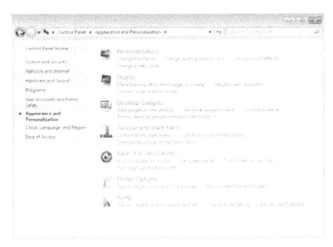

Figure 4.19

In Figure 4.20 you see the different options for configuring your desktop, background, colors, sound, and the screen saver.

Setting Backgrounds

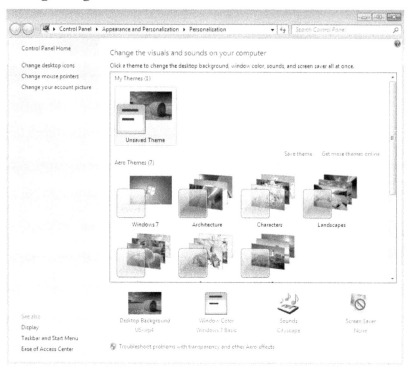

Figure 4.20

You can click on any of the pictures to make them your desktop background or choose your own. In Figure 4.21 you will see the Windows colors and appearance options that you can choose instead of a picture for your background.

Setting Colors and Appearance

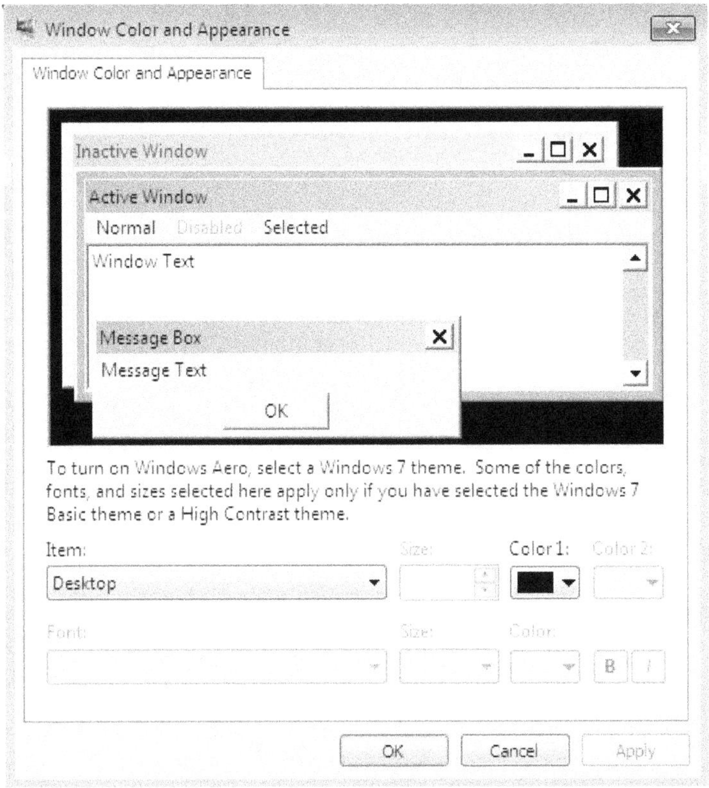

Figure 4.21

Let's say you want to stop the Windows login music, or change your beeps to a dog bark. How would you do that? Well make it a .WAV file and change the sounds until you find one you like, as shown in Figure 4.22. You can also choose to use themes you have downloaded or that come preconfigured in Windows 7.

Sound Settings

Figure 4.22

Screen savers keep your screens from getting burned in images that you can see as shadows when you are using your computer. These are caused by the same screen burning the pixels from being in too long. In Figure 4.23 you will see where you can change the screensaver and the settings.

Configuring Screen Saver Settings

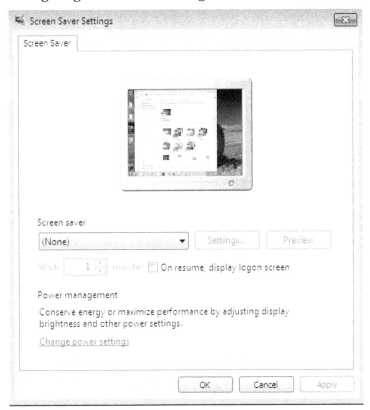

Figure 4.23

Configuring Desktop Icons

Figure 4.24

Many of these icons were on the desktop by default in Windows 98 and
Windows 2000. In XP and Vista these icons were there in Classic Mode or by
selection. In Windows 7 they are here only by selecting them in this screen. By
placing a checkmark as shown in Figure 4.24 on any of these boxes the
corresponding icon will show up on the desktop.

Changing the Mouse Pointer Properties

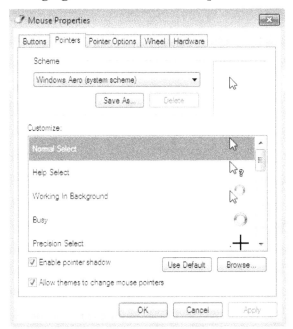

Figure 4.25

The screen shown in Figure 4.25, allows you to change the properties of your mouse. This includes customizing the pointer, effects, buttons, sensitivity and much more.

Change Your Profile Picture

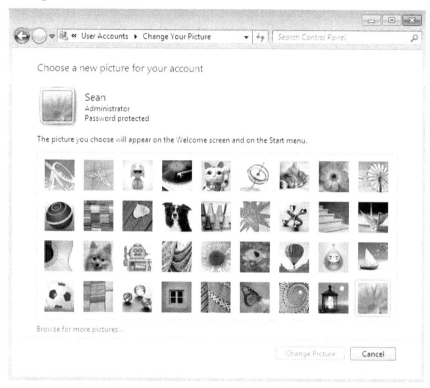

Figure 4.26

This screen shown in Figure 4.26 allows you to change your profile picture to any of the preinstalled pictures or to browse for more pictures or search for your own.

Change Your Display Settings

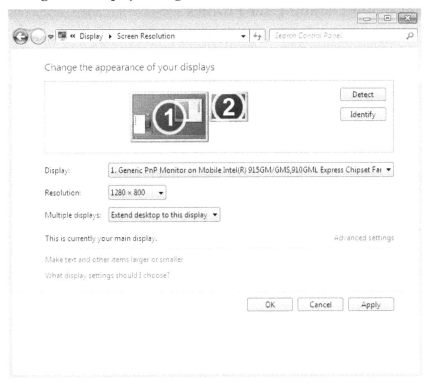

Figure 4.27

The screen in Figure 4.27 shows the different options for adjusting your screen size, adding a second monitor, and adjusting the advanced settings. For more information on the advanced setting please see:

http://www.sevenforums.com/tutorials/258-color-bit-depth-display-settings.html

Customizing Default User Profiles

You can customize the default user profile during an unattended installation using the following Copy Profile parameter in the Unattend.xml answer file that is passed to the Sysprep.exe. To do this, follow these steps:

1. Use the administrator account or an account that has administrative privileges to log on to the computer.

2. Configure the settings that you want to use in the profile. This includes desktop settings, favorites, and Start menu options.

3. Create an Unattend.xml file that contains the Copy Profile parameter. By using this Copy Profile parameter, the settings of the user who is currently logged on are copied to the default user profile. This parameter must be set to "true" in the specialize pass. For example, the parameter must be as follows:

   <CopyProfile>true</CopyProfile>

4. You can use the Windows System Image Manager tool to create the Unattend.xml file. The Windows System Image Manager tool is included as part of the Windows Automated Installation Kit (Windows AIK). For more information about Windows AIK, visit the following Microsoft Web site:

   http://technet.microsoft.com/en-us/library/dd349343.aspx

5. Choose Start and type CMD at the search prompt or at a command prompt, type the following command:

   sysprep.exe /generalize /unattend: unattend.xml

6. Open Sysprep.exe which is located in the %systemdrive%\Windows\System32\sysprep directory.

7. You must use the /generalize switch so that the Copy Profile parameter can be used. The /unattend is an optional syntax which is used to point to the desired Unattend.xml file.

8. **Note:** The Unattend.xml file is located in the sysprep directory.

Copy a User Profile to a Network Default User Profile

Now that we have learned these steps, let's learn how to turn the default user profile into a network default user profile in Windows 7 using the following steps.

1. Log on to the computer that has the customized default user profile by using an account that has administrative privileges.

2. Use the Run command to connect to the NETLOGON shared folder of a domain controller. For example, the path resembles the following:

   \\<*Server_name*>*NETLOGON*

3. Create a new folder in the NETLOGON shared folder, and name it Default User.v2.

4. Click Start from the Start menu, right-click Computer, click Properties, and then click Advanced system settings.

5. Under User Profiles, click Settings. The User Profiles dialog box shows a list of profiles that are stored on the computer.

6. Select Default Profile, and then click Copy To.

7. In the Copy profile to text box, type the network path of the Windows 7 default user profile folder that you created in step 3. For example, type the following path:

8. \\<Server_name>\NETLOGON\Default User.v2

9. Under Permitted to use, click Change, type the name Everyone group, and then click OK.

10. Click OK to start to copy the profile.

11. Log off the computer when the copying process is completed.

Chapter 5 - Super Bar (Task Bar)

In this book I tend to call the Taskbar, the Start Bar several places as many people can understand what I am talking about. However, many people at Microsoft and on the Internet are referring to Windows 7 version as the "Superbar". So from here on out I will try to refer to it as the Superbar.

In Microsoft texts the Taskbar is still named "Taskbar" in Windows 7. Let's take a look at this new bar in Figure 5.1 which you will immediately notice is much glassier look than previous versions of Windows.

Figure 5.1

Like Vista's task bar, the Windows 7 taskbar also provides a preview of the running applications by using their running icons by default. Also there is a small sliver bar next to each icon which allows you to view multiple instances of that application. So if you have two word documents open you can view and then select the one you want to see as shown in Figure 5.2.

Figure 5.2

In the rest of this chapter I am going to walk you through customizing the Superbar, the Superbar options, the features of the Superbar, and some Group Policy Edits.

Customizing the Superbar Properties

If we right click on the round Windows 7 logo or the Superbar we get two and select Properties you will see the options in Figure 5.3. We will then select the Toolbar Tab to add some additional features to our Superbar. In Figure 5.3 you will see I have right clicked on the Superbar and chosen Properties. In the Toolbars Tab I have checked the Address tab and clicked Apply. In Figure 5.4 you will see the changes this has made to the Superbar.

Figure 5.3

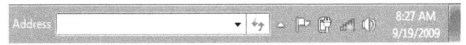

Figure 5.4

Next, I will check the Link option and press apply. In Figure 5.5 you will see the Link option on the Superbar to the left and the menu that appears when you get when you click the Link option.

Figure 5.5

The next option is for those who use Windows 7 on a Tablet PC. But if you have a but don't use a Tablet PC, it is fun to use your mouse or a graphics tablet to play with it and try and convert what you write to actual typed text. In Figure 5.6 you will see I have now checked the Tablet PC option and pressed apply. I have then clicked on the new option on the bar which brings up the Tablet PC menu box.

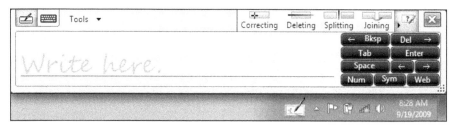

Figure 5.6

The last option is the Desktop option which places all your shortcuts and folders from your desktop onto the menu. An arrow to the left gives you the additional files or folders which are contained on the desktop. Also the folders contained in your Documents folder are also listed. Also you have shortcuts to My Computer, the Network, and the Control Panel all accessible in one easy place as shown in Figure 5.7.

Figure 5.7

Show Desktop Button

This is one of my favorite icons in the taskbar. It has got a slightly different location in the new Superbar right next to the clock. This new feature is different from the old Desktop Icon which minimized all your open application windows. If you had 8 windows open, you had to click each one to maximize them again after pressing the old Desktop Icon.

This new button as shown in Figure 5.8 minimizes all of your open application windows which are maximized on the screen. When you are done looking at your desktop, simply click the button again and walla, all of your windows are back open just the way they were before.

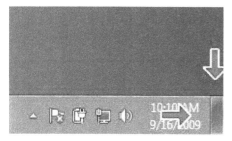

Figure 5.8

Using the Superbar Customize Feature

Figure 5.9

In Figure 5.9 above you will notice the little up arrow on the Superbar by the clock. You can also see that I have clicked on this arrow and it has given me options. There are other shortcuts at the top which are Superbar icons I do not want to see on the Superbar. But let's say I did want to see them all or one or more of these on the Superbar. I would click the Customize option.

In Figure 5.10, you will see each Icon I have available and a drop down menu next to each of them giving you three options. These options are:

- Show icon and notifications
- Hide icon and notifications
- Only Show notifications

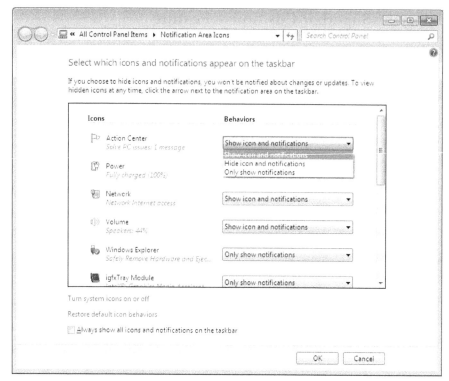

Figure 5.10

If I want to see all of the Icons on the menu bar I would simply click on Always show all icons and notifications on the taskbar and click OK as shown on Figure 5.11. You will notice the changes on the Superbar where it now shows all the icons.

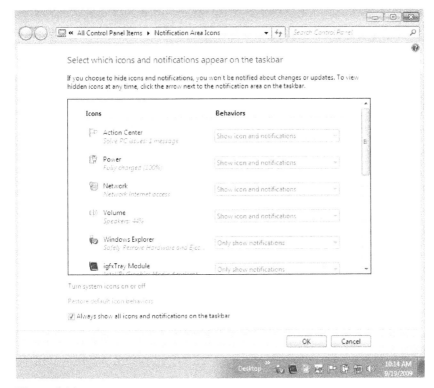

Figure 5.11

Windows Aero Overview

Aero is a new feature introduced in Windows Vista and expanded in Windows 7 to improve the desktop look and experience. Aero requires a display adapter compatible with Windows Display Driver Model (WDDM) and a Windows 7 Windows Experience Index of 3.0 or better to work. We will talk about how to view these options later in this section.

First though let's get a look at the items we will focus on in this section which are:

- **Aero Glass**
- **Aero Peek**
- **Aero Snap**
- **Aero Shake**
- **Windows Flip 3D**

In most circumstance, if the PC's display card satisfies the minimum requirement to run Windows Aero, which appears to be not much different, to what's required in Windows Vista:

1. 1 GHz 32-bit (x86) or 64-bit (x64) processor
2. 1 GB (gigabyte) of RAM memory
3. DirectX 9 compatible GPU with a minimum of 128 MB of Video RAM
4. Windows Display Driver Model (WDDM) driver
5. Windows 7 will automatically enable Windows Aero upon installation.

Alert: *Aero is not a feature of Windows 7 Starter Edition.*

Sometimes Windows Aero may not be turned on, or is having problem to enable. This is for many reasons such unsupported video drivers, outdated or unsupported VGA graphic display card, not meeting the above requirements, or Windows 7 just does not automatically enable. Let's take a look at how to find out what is wrong and see if we can get Windows 7 to enable this feature with the instructions in the next section.

How to Enable Aero in Windows 7

1. Once you have finished Installing Windows 7 install updated video drivers for your windows 7.

2. Refresh your WEI (Windows Experience Index) Score. In order to refresh WEI right on My Computer -> Properties, A New window with System information will be displayed as shown in Figure 5.12.

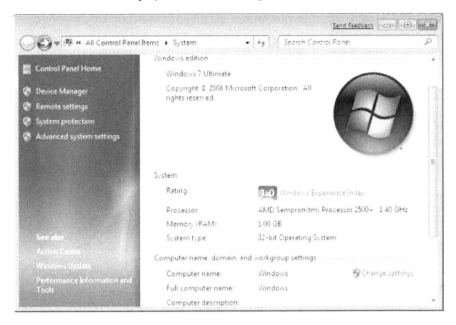

Figure 5.12

3. Click on Performance Information and Tools at the bottom right side of window and view your PC's WEI Score as shown in Figure 5.13. A score of 3.0 or better is required for Windows 7 to automatically enable this feature.

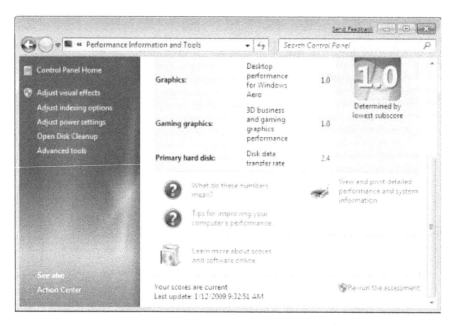

Figure 5.13

4. Now click Re-run the assessment

(Or you can simply Click on start->type **cmd** and type following command: **winsat formal)**

Once your Windows Experience Index is recalculated and if it's higher then 3.0, Aero in Windows 7 will Aero Glass will automatically be enabled.

> **NOTE:** You *can change colors by right clicking on desktop-> Personalize -> Select Windows Colors.*

Aero Peek Feature

Aero Peak is the new and improved thumbnail previews added to the Superbar. This is very important when you want to switch between applications when you have multiple windows open. You might need to minimize every other window opened to look for your application. You can also use ALT + TAB or use Windows Flip 3D to browse the applications.

With the new Superbar, you can just hover on the thumbnail previews to get a preview of that window while the other windows fade away into glass sheets and easily switch to your application!

Aero Snap Feature

There is also a really cool feature which allows you to drag an application to the left or right until the screen dims as shown in Figure 5.14. When you release, your application will be exactly half the screen width.

Figure 5.14

Note: *The Windows Key + the right arrow key will produce the same result.*

It's a great way of comparing documents side by side as shown in Figure 5.15.

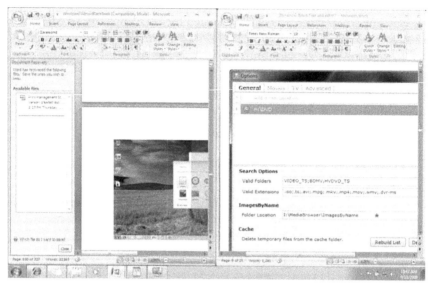

Figure 5.15

Aero Shake Feature

Aero Shake is a new feature to help wear out your mouse quicker so that manufacturers of mice can start upping their sales counts. I am just kidding. What Aero Shake does is allows you to shake an application on your desktop by clicking at the top and moving quickly left and right. By doing this all the other windows you have opened except for the one you are moving left and right will quickly minimize.

It's a nice feature that I can see some practical use for, but I think they need to work on the sensitivity so users don't wear out their mice. Of course it does have some exercise value. Maybe they should call it the "Microsoft Fit" function. I mean Wii came out with their version.

Aero Glass Feature

Aero Glass effect is one of new features of Windows Vista and is now extended to Windows 7. It features a translucent glass design with sublet windows animations and new windows colors.

The Aero Glass effects all of your open application windows makes them transparent like glass as shown below in Figure 5.16.

Figure 5.16

Windows Flip 3D

Windows Flip improves on the ALT+TAB method for flipping between application windows; while Windows Flip 3D dynamically displays all open windows in a graceful three-dimensional view as shown in Figure 5.17 which shows the results of hovering over the Internet Explorer icon on the Superbar.

Windows Flip 3D uses the dimension of visual depth to give you a more comprehensive view of your open windows, helping you sidestep chaos even as you juggle myriad open files and programs.

Windows Flip 3D can even render images of live processes such as currently playing video. Use the START+TAB keys to initiate the 3-D view, then flip through open windows by using arrow keys or the scroll wheel on your mouse to quickly identify and select the one you want. Navigating your desktop has never been this fun.

Figure 5.17

Troubleshooting Windows Aero

Whatever the cause of your Windows Aero failure, there is the easy way to fix all issues, bugs or problems related to Windows Aero, and then turn on and enable the Windows Aero feature in Windows 7. We discussed a way up in the Windows Aero Overview but thanks to a new troubleshooting task tool added in Windows 7 even easier.

To troubleshoot Aero effects such as transparency in Windows 7, follow these steps:

1. Make sure that **Windows Experience Index** has been calculated and computed.

2. Click on **Start** menu.

3. Type the following text into the Start Search box:

   Aero

4. Click on the search result listing under Control Panel group named, "Find and fix problems with transparency and other visual effects". Right click and choose Open. The result is displayed in Figure 5.18.

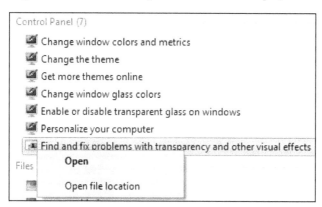

Figure 5.18

Note: *If you don't see "Find and fix problems with transparency and other visual effects" in the search results, click on Control Panel option displayed in the results to see all Aero related.*

5. Next an "Aero – Troubleshooting Computer Problems" wizard will appear. Click on **Next** button. As shown in Figure 5.19. After clicking Next you will see the screen shown in Figure 5.20.

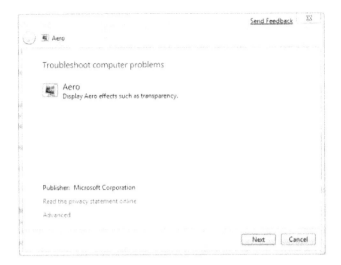

Figure 5.19

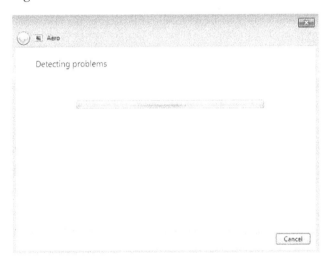

Figure 5.20

6. The troubleshooting wizard will attempt to detect any problems by running a series of checks as shown in Figure 5.21.

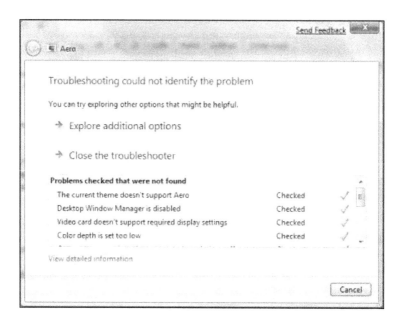

Figure 5.21

Alert: *Items with a red cross which indicates a problem which may prevent Aero from working properly, fix the issues and then rerun the "Find and fix problems with transparency and other visual effects" troubleshooting wizard again.*

Note: *There are also other registry hacks available on the Internet to force Aero to work as long as your display card supports WDDI. I actually created a whole chapter on these hacks but the Editor of this book, as well as the Technical Editor voiced concerns about it. So it got removed. But you can Bing or Google, "Aero Hacks" and you will find them. Also note though, that if you do something to screw up your PC by using these hacks, Microsoft will most likely not help you fix it.*

Other Superbar Features and Customizations

In this section let's talk about some other cool features and customizations that can be made to the Superbar. We will take a look at the following items:

- Group Policy Editor customizations
- Identifying open and closed applications
- Application progress bars
- Application Previews
- Pin and unpin applications to the Superbar
- Customizing the Superbar With The Taskbar Properties Taskbar Tab

Group Policy Editor Customizations

There are a number of customizations that can be made to the Superbar from the Group Policy Editor. So many in fact that I realized I could write an entire book just on this subject. So I am going to show you how to turn off the taskbar thumbnails on the Superbar. Then on your own you can scroll through the different items you can modify until your heart is content. I counted 355 options under the Start Menu. It might be more or less depending on your Windows 7 version.

So how you enable or disable thumbnail previews in Windows 7 is follow these instructions:

1. Click on start and type on search bar **gpedit.msc** and press enter

2. Now navigate to **User Configuration, Administrative Templates,** and **Start Menu and Taskbar** in left window of the Group Policy Editor as shown in Figure 5.22. You will notice in the right window all of the options I talked about before.

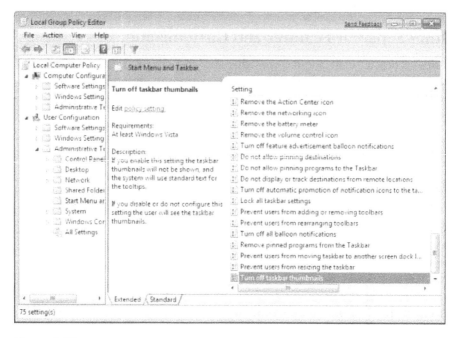

Figure 5.22

3. Locate **"Turn off Taskbar Thumbnails"** in right window of the Group policy editor and double click on it.

4. Select Disable and then click apply as shown in Figure 5.23.

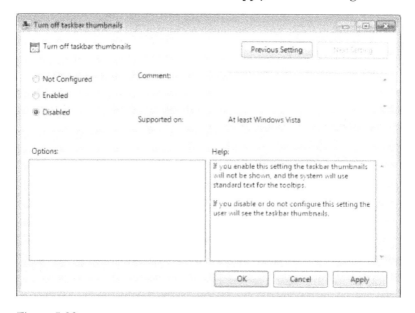

Figure 5.23

5. Now check your Taskbar. You should now show just the file names instead of pictures.

Application Progress Bars

The application progress bars for downloading from the Internet or saving applications is actually a new unique feature. As shown below in Figure 5.24, you will see Internet Explorer downloading a PDF and a search that I have running. The search is at 36% and the download is at 48%. I need to note that only some applications provide progress bars. Not all.

Figure 5.24

One item that became apparent to me is that when I had multiple instances of downloads in Internet Explorer it becomes difficult to keep track of multiple progresses in the same application. If you hover your mouse over the applications Icon on the Superbar however, you can get a more accurate look at where the progress is on each individual

Pin and Unpin Applications to the Superbar

Unlike earlier versions of Windows you can now very easy go to Pin and Unpin icons to the Superbar. This is a way to keep your most used application shortcuts right on the Superbar . The Pin to Taskbar is available if you right click and application in the Start menu, Programs menu, or right off an open application already in the Superbar. In Figure 5.25, I am pinning Microsoft Word to the Superbar using the Pin to Taskbar option. You will note I can also choose to pin the application to the Start Menu where I am getting the Windows Word shortcut from.

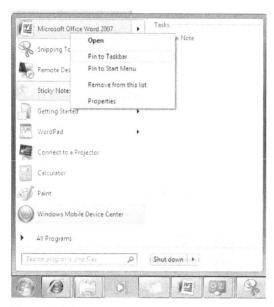

Figure 5.25

Now that it is pinned to the Superbar anytime I log out or restart the computer the Microsoft Word shortcut and icon will be displayed in the Superbar. If I right click on the Microsoft Word icon in the Superbar I will have the option of Unpinning the program as shown in Figure 5.26.

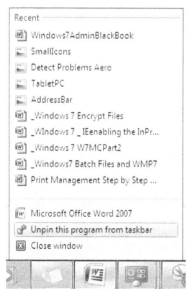

Figure 5.26

Taskbar and Start Menu Properties Taskbar Tab

Occasionally, some users might not like the new way of grouping items, especially the icon overlay display where sometimes it becomes difficult for some users to identify which applications are running and closed.

You can easily access these options in the Taskbar properties dialog window as shown in Figure 5.27.

Figure 5.27

Below there are screenshots of taskbar buttons with different options as shown in Figures 5.28, 5.29, and 5.30.:

1) Always combine, hide labels (default behavior)

Figure 5.28

2) Combine when taskbar is full (similar to earlier versions of Windows)

Figure 5.29

3) Using small icons

Figure 5.30

The Superbar is indeed a major feature update for Windows 7. Of course, many users will find the Superbar initially surprising as it needs some time to grasp the new features, but once you become familiar with the Superbar, you will start enjoying the simplicity of the new evolved Windows Taskbar.

Windows Key Shortcuts

Windows 7 has significantly more Windows key shortcuts than any Windows version before. Let's take a look at what Windows key combinations you can use to save yourself time. For those of you with a laptop without a Windows key. I feel sorry for you.

Key Combination	What It Does
Windows key +ESC	Open or close the Start menu.
Windows key +Pause	Display the System Properties dialog box.
Windows key +D	Display the desktop.
Windows key +M	Minimize all windows.
Windows key +Shift+M	Restore minimized windows to the desktop.
Windows key +E	Open Computer.
Windows key +F	Search for a file or folder.
Ctrl+Windows key +F	Search for computers (if you're on a network).
Windows key +L	Lock your computer or switch users.
Windows key +R	Open the Run dialog box.
Windows key +T	Cycle through programs on the taskbar.

Windows key +number	Start the program pinned to the taskbar in the position indicated by the number.
Shift+Windows key +number	Start a new instance of the program pinned to the taskbar in the position number.
Ctrl+Windows key number	Switch to the last active window of the program + pinned to the taskbar in the number.
Alt+Windows key +number	Open the Jump List for the program pinned to the taskbar in the position number
Windows key	Cycle through programs on the taskbar by using **+Tab** Aero Flip 3-D.
Ctrl+Windows key	Use the arrow keys to cycle through programs **+Tab** on the taskbar by using Aero Flip 3-D.
Ctrl+Windows key	Switch to the program that displayed a message **+B** in the notification area.
Windows key +Spacebar	Preview the desktop.
Windows key +Up Arrow	Maximize the window.
Windows key Arrow screen.	Maximize the window to the left side of the **+Left**
Windows key Arrow screen.	Maximize the window to the right side of the **+Right**
Windows key +Down Arrow	Minimize the window.
Windows key +Home	Minimize all but the active window.
Windows key +Shift+Up Arrow	Stretch the window to the top and bottom of the screen.
Windows key +P	Choose a presentation display mode.

Windows key +G	Cycle through gadgets.
Windows key +U	Open Ease of Access Center.
Windows key +X	Open Windows Mobility Center.

Chapter 6 – File Security and Encryption

Windows 7 is full of ways to protect yourself when you are using your computer. There are so many threats out there that it is important to be proactive and educated on possible threats to your computer and do what you can to detect and prevent them.

In this section we will show you how to keep applications off your network PC's, how to encrypt your sensitive data, and how to protect your privacy when using Windows Media Player included with your Windows 7 operating system.

AppLocker

AppLocker as shown in Figure 6.1, it is a new application control feature available in Microsoft Windows 7 that helps eliminate unwanted and unknown applications within an organization's network to providing a much more productive and secure environment.

Figure 6.1

These screens are blown up in the next few pages so don't go grab your magnifying glass just yet.

AppLocker answers the need for application control with a simple and flexible application that allows administrators to specify exactly what is allowed to run on the computer in their network environment. There are many benefits to using AppLocker in your network such as:

- Stop unlicensed software from being installed or run in your environment.
- Preventing vulnerable, unauthorized applications from being installed or run in your environment.
- Prevent user from running applications which waste time.
- Stopping users from running applications that needlessly consume network bandwidth.
- Preventing users from running applications that possible contain viruses or malware.
- Allow users to install and run software and updates based upon their business needs
- Ensure compliance of corporate policies and industry regulations for PCI DSS, Sarbanes-Oxley, HIPAA, Basel II, and state identity theft protection acts.
- Reduce the cost of repair for users who install software which causes their PC to have issues or infects other devices in the network.

AppLocker provides a powerful solution using three rule types: allow, deny, and exception. Allow rules limit execution of applications to a "good list" of programs and applications. Deny rules take the opposite approach and disallow all programs and applications on the "bad list". Exception rules allow you to exclude files from an allow/deny rule that would normally be included such as a rule to "allow everything in the Windows Operating System to run, except the built-in games."

AppLocker is configured in the Group Policy Editor in Local Computer Policy, Security Settings, Application Control Policies, and then AppLocker as shown in Figure 6.2. In Figure 6.3 you will see the options that you can configure for AppLocker.

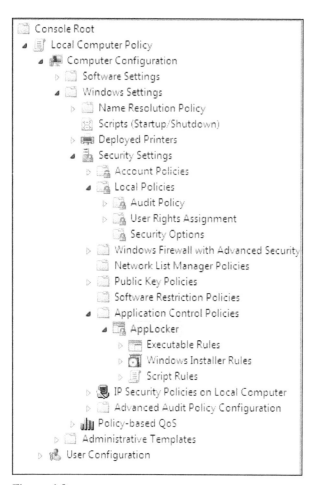

Figure 6.2

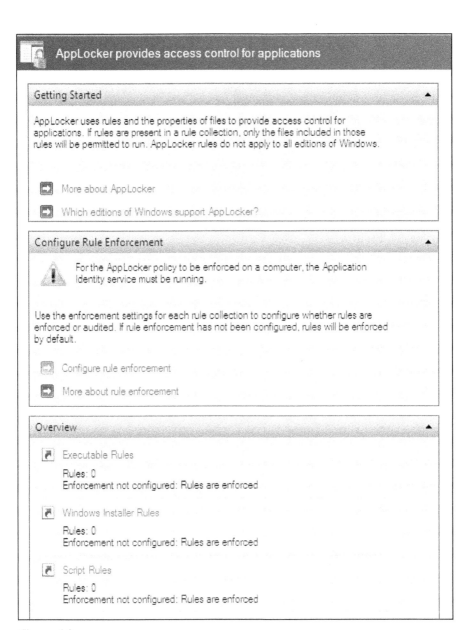

Figure 6.3

User Access Control (UAC)

To access UAC settings click the Start button, type *UAC,* and click on Change User Account Control Settings. This page is relatively simple with only four options to decide the level of security you want associated with your profile. These options range from never notify to always notify.

Figures 6.4, 6.5, 6.6, and 6.7 show the four options available and when you will receive an alert. The default is shown in Figure 6.4.

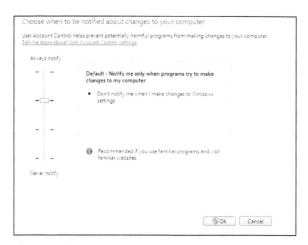

Figure 6.4

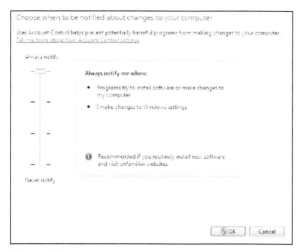

Figure 6.5

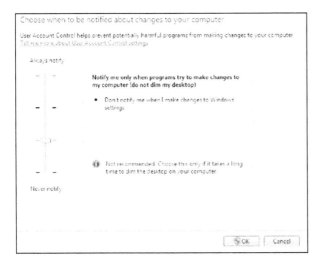

Figure 6.6

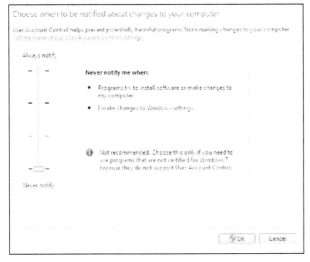

Figure 6.7

BitLocker

BitLocker drive encryption is a new feature that provides protection for operating hard drives, external drives, and removable data drives in case they are lost or stolen. BitLocker is a way of encrypting the data on drives and requiring authentication to access the information.

BitLocker encrypts your drives so others cannot access them without a password. BitLocker comes in two flavors in Windows 7 which are BitLocker and BitLock To Go.

You can also force the PC to book from an encryption key on a USB flash drive. You can insert the USB flash drive into the computer during startup to allow it to book. The USB flash drive is used to unlock the computer.

When enabling BitLocker on a hard drive or removable drives, BitLocker can use the following unlock methods:

> Password: You can use a password to unlock your BitLocker encrypted data drives and Group Policy settings can be used to set minimum password lengths.

> Smart card: BitLocker allows you to use a compatible certificate on your smart card. By default, BitLocker will choose the certificate unless you have multiple compatible certificates, in which case you must choose the certificate to use.

BitLocker To Go was specially created to encrypt the data on your portable media. With an increasing number of key drives being used, the loss of sensitive data is becoming more of a threat.

Encrypting Your Thumb Drive

To encrypt your thumb drive, do the following you should plug your thumb drive into a USB port, click the Start button, type BitLocker, and click on BitLocker Drive Encryption. Next to your drive letter of your thumb drive, click Turn on BitLocker as shown in Figure 6.8.

Choose a password and click Continue as shown in Figure 6.9. You will be given the option to save your recovery key (used if you forget your password) or print it. If you save the file, ensure the file is stored somewhere safe and then click Next as shown in Figure 6.10.

You will then need to confirm your chosen settings, the password and click Start Encrypting as shown in Figure 6.11.

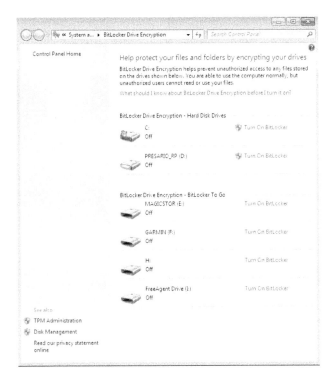

Figure 6.8

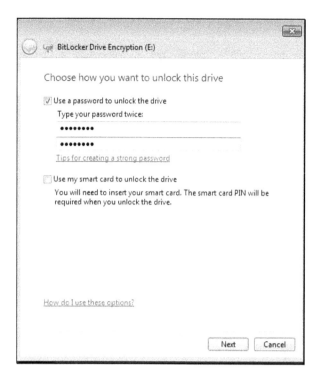

Figure 6.9

Figure 6.10

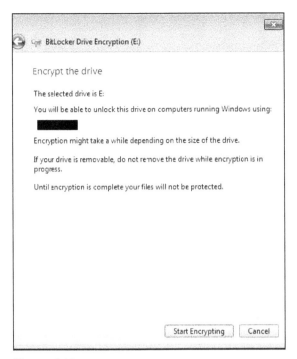

Figure 6.11

After you click Start Encrypting you will see the screen in Figure 6.12. Please notice the Figure above where it warns that large drives may take quite a while.

Starting encryption

⚠ Do not remove your drive until encryption begins.

Figure 6.12

Now that I am done, I am going to try and access the drive I just encrypted. As soon as I try a new screen appears asking me to enter a password before I can access the drive as shown in Figure 6.13.

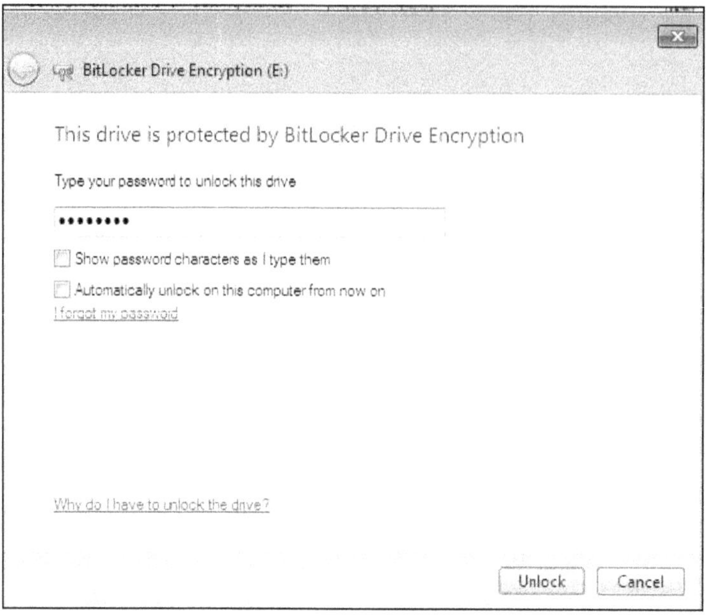

Figure 6.13

Setting up Your Homegroup

Homegroup is a new feature in Windows 7 that makes it easy to share your libraries and printers on a home network. Homegroup provides password protection and a choice of what you want to share with others.

A Homegroup is created in the Control Panel under the Network and Internet as shown in Figure 6.14.

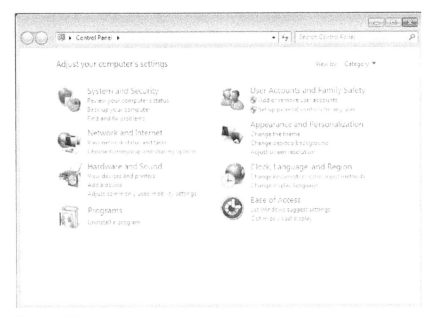

Figure 6.14

You will see the options for the Network and Internet settings as shown in Figure 6.15. The second option called Homegroup is where you create or remove a Homegroup or make changes to the settings.

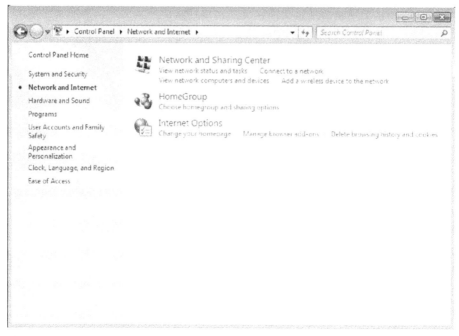

Figure 6.15

If no Homegroup is configured, the first screen you will see is the one pictured in Figure 6.16.

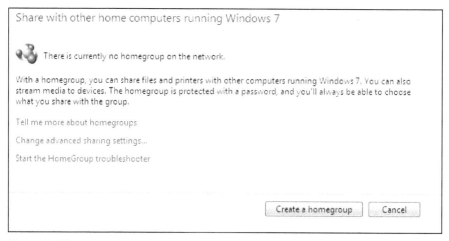

Figure 6.16

Once you select Create a Homegroup, the next screen as shown in Figure 6.17 allows you to decide which items you will be sharing with others by clicking the box and placing a checkmark next to the option. Choose from Pictures, Documents, Printers, Music, and Videos.

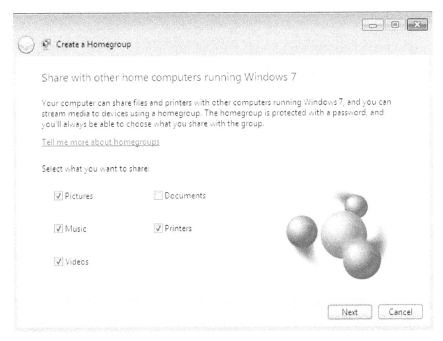

Figure 6.17

Next, Windows will automatically prepare your Homegroup for you. Once this part is done, you will need to get a shared password, which allows other computers, running Windows 7, to connect to your Homegroup. Figure 6.18 shows the screen where you are given your password.

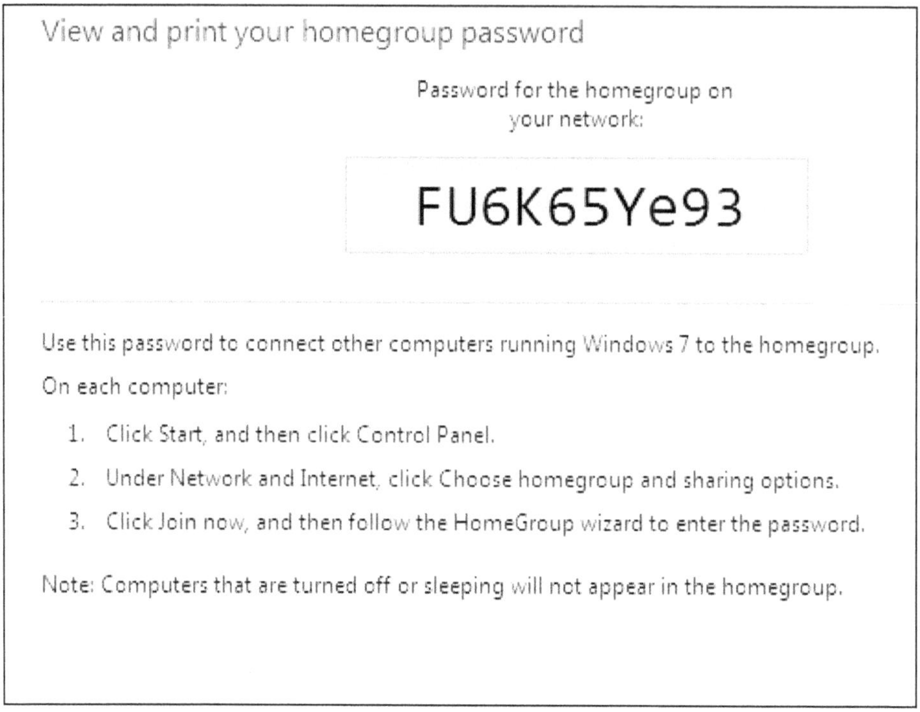

View and print your homegroup password

Password for the homegroup on
your network:

FU6K65Ye93

Use this password to connect other computers running Windows 7 to the homegroup.
On each computer:

1. Click Start, and then click Control Panel.
2. Under Network and Internet, click Choose homegroup and sharing options.
3. Click Join now, and then follow the HomeGroup wizard to enter the password.

Note: Computers that are turned off or sleeping will not appear in the homegroup.

Figure 6.18

The password is also available to view whenever you need by going back to the Homegroup link in Network and Sharing as shown in Figure 6.19.

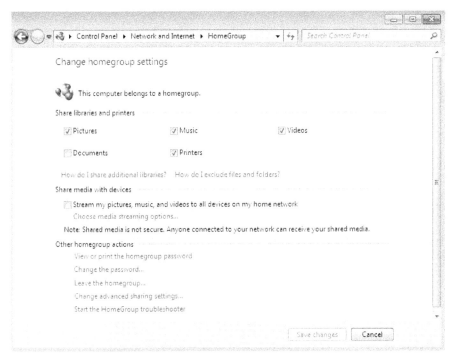

Figure 6.19

Note: *Joining a Homegroup is easy. To join your current Homegroup, go to your second PC and connect to the same network (wireless or wired) the Homegroup is configured on. You will automatically be prompted to join the Homegroup. Click "Join Now" and type in your Homegroup password.*

Encrypting NTFS using the Cipher Tool

The Cipher Tool, displays or alters the encryption of directories and files on NTFS volumes. If used without parameters, cipher displays the encryption state of the current directory and any files it contains.

The tools syntaxes are shown in Figures 6.19 and 6.20.

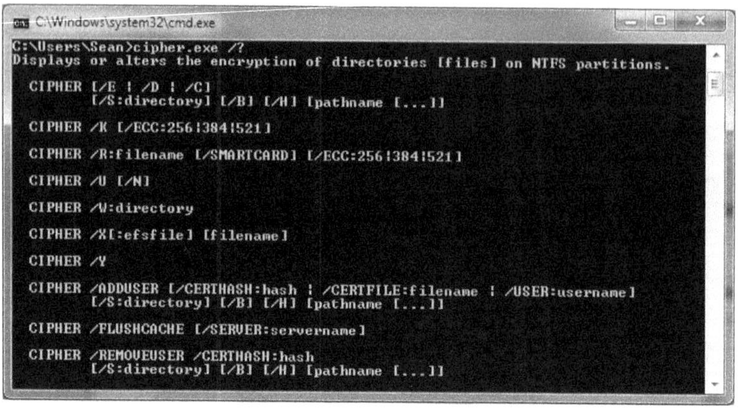

```
C:\Windows\system32\cmd.exe

C:\Users\Sean>cipher.exe /?
Displays or alters the encryption of directories [files] on NTFS partitions.

    CIPHER [/E | /D | /C]
           [/S:directory] [/B] [/H] [pathname [...]]

    CIPHER /K [/ECC:256|384|521]

    CIPHER /R:filename [/SMARTCARD] [/ECC:256|384|521]

    CIPHER /U [/N]

    CIPHER /W:directory

    CIPHER /X[:efsfile] [filename]

    CIPHER /Y

    CIPHER /ADDUSER [/CERTHASH:hash | /CERTFILE:filename | /USER:username]
           [/S:directory] [/B] [/H] [pathname [...]]

    CIPHER /FLUSHCACHE [/SERVER:servername]

    CIPHER /REMOVEUSER /CERTHASH:hash
           [/S:directory] [/B] [/H] [pathname [...]]
```

Figure 6.20

154

```
CIPHER /REMOVEUSER /CERTHASH:hash
        [/S:directory] [/B] [/H] [pathname [...]]

CIPHER /REKEY [pathname [...]]

        /B      Abort if an error is encountered. By default, CIPHER continues
                executing even if errors are encountered.
        /C      Displays information on the encrypted file.
        /D      Decrypts the specified files or directories.
        /E      Encrypts the specified files or directories. Directories will be
                marked so that files added afterward will be encrypted. The
                encrypted file could become decrypted when it is modified if the
                parent directory is not encrypted. It is recommended that you
                encrypt the file and the parent directory.
        /H      Displays files with the hidden or system attributes. These files
                are omitted by default.
        /K      Creates a new certificate and key for use with EFS. If this
                option is chosen, all the other options will be ignored.

                Note: By default, /K creates a certificate and key that conform
                      to current group policy. If ECC is specified, a self-signed
                      certificate will be created with the supplied key size.

        /N      This option only works with /U. This will prevent keys being
                updated. This is used to find all the encrypted files on the
                local drives.
        /R      Generates an EFS recovery key and certificate, then writes them
                to a .PFX file (containing certificate and private key) and a
                .CER file (containing only the certificate). An administrator may
                add the contents of the .CER to the EFS recovery policy to create
                the recovery key for users, and import the .PFX to recover
                individual files. If SMARTCARD is specified, then writes the
                recovery key and certificate to a smart card. A .CER file is
                generated (containing only the certificate). No .PFX file is
                generated.

                Note: By default, /R creates an 2048-bit RSA recovery key and
                      certificate. If ECC is specified, it must be followed by a
                      key size of 256, 384, or 521.

        /S      Performs the specified operation on the given directory and all
                files and subdirectories within it.
        /U      Tries to touch all the encrypted files on local drives. This will
                update user's file encryption key or recovery keys to the current
                ones if they are changed. This option does not work with other
                options except /N.
        /W      Removes data from available unused disk space on the entire
                volume. If this option is chosen, all other options are ignored.
                The directory specified can be anywhere in a local volume. If it
                is a mount point or points to a directory in another volume, the
                data on that volume will be removed.
        /X      Backup EFS certificate and keys into file filename. If efsfile is
                provided, the current user's certificate(s) used to encrypt the
                file will be backed up. Otherwise, the user's current EFS
                certificate and keys will be backed up.
        /Y      Displays your current EFS certificate thumbnail on the local PC.
     /ADDUSER   Adds a user to the specified encrypted file(s). If CERTHASH is
                provided, cipher will search for a certificate with this SHA1
                hash. If CERTFILE is provided, cipher will extract the
                certificate from the file. If USER is provided, cipher will
                try to locate the user's certificate in Active Directory Domain
                Services.
     /FLUSHCACHE
                Clears the calling user's EFS key cache on the specified server.
                If servername is not provided, cipher clears the user's key cache
                on the local machine.
     /REKEY     Updates the specified encrypted file(s) to use the configured
                EFS current key.
     /REMOVEUSER
                Removes a user from the specified file(s). CERTHASH must be the
                SHA1 hash of the certificate to remove.

     directory  A directory path.
     filename   A filename without extensions.
     pathname   Specifies a pattern, file or directory.
     efsfile    An encrypted file path.

Used without parameters, CIPHER displays the encryption state of the
current directory and any files it contains. You may use multiple directory
names and wildcards. You must put spaces between multiple parameters.

C:\Users\Sean>
```

Figure 6.20

In Figure 6.21 you see the tool configured to wipe the free(swap) space on the drive and overwrite it with random characters.

Figure 6.21

There are many syntax for this command. For more information visit:

http://technet.microsoft.com/en-us/library/ee424301(WS.10).aspx

Chapter 7 – Maintaining Windows 7

In a perfect world your computer would never break, never need maintenance, never slow down, never get a virus, and never lose any of your data. Well this computer you have and the operating system are very technical and they have a lot of moving parts. Not to mention the environment you place it in can be just as bad as anything else. One of my customers has about 20 employees, but he runs a machine shop and my technicians are out there every other week performing maintenance on the PC's and they still break down. Also just using your PC, moving files, doing searches, and just about anything you do with your PC creates a need for regular maintenance.

If there wasn't a need to fix and maintain Windows PC's and servers, there wouldn't be a platoon of certified people out there to work on them. You would take the PC out of the box, it would be ready to go and you would never have a need to call technical support, or fix anything. It would be a perfect world. Well it's not so you better continue reading this chapter.

Let's take a look at what we will cover in this chapter some more features of the Action Center such as:

- Windows Update

- Windows Defragmenter

- Windows Disk Cleanup

- Windows Check Disk (CHKDSK)

- Windows Backup

Note: *Regardless of the version of Windows 7 you have purchased. All the features in this chapter are in included.*

System Security with Windows Updates

To get bugs in the operating system fixed automatically, stay safe on a network and the Internet you need to keep your system up to date. In this day and age it is absolutely essential step in maintaining a secure computer environment. When threats emerge, Windows has been quick to patch and make changes to their operating system to quickly fix the issue. This has been thanks to the Windows Update program which has been completely redesigned in Windows 7. The Windows Update setting page available in the Windows Action Center allows you to configure your Windows Update settings as shown in Figure 7.1.

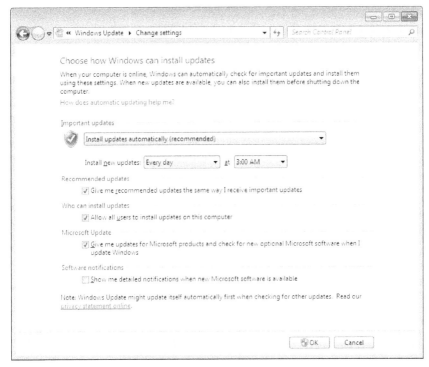

Figure 7.1

Microsoft routinely releases security updates on the second Tuesday of each month on what s known as, "Patch Tuesday". Most other Microsoft updates are when the need arises, such as when a fix is developed for a newly discovered problem. If you keep the settings at the default setting, updates will install automatically.

The Change Settings dialog box lets you specify how you want Windows Updates to operate. The options allow you to specify whether to download and let you specify which ones to install, specify which updates to install and then download, or just disable Windows Updates all together as shown in Figure 7.2.

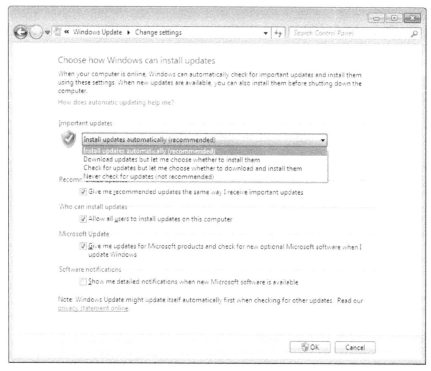

Figure 7.2

If you use the Install Updates Automatically (Recommended) option Windows will come out of sleep mode automatically at the time you selected and update your system. If you have either the "download, but don't install" or "check, but don't download or install" options selected, Windows Update notifies you with a flag notification when new updates are available for you to approve. This is very time consuming and not recommended.

"Who Can Install Updates", allows an administrator of the PC to either allow all users to install updates or uncheck the box to allow only administrators to install updates.

"Microsoft Update", if checked it allows you to update for other Microsoft products other than the operating system and also install software that Microsoft recommends.

"Software Notifications", this gives you detailed information of the updates Microsoft has installed. If you have ever gone to Microsoft's update website and installed updates you see a reason, what the update does for you and the Microsoft identification code.

Sidebar: What if an update gives me trouble?

If you suspect a particular update creates a problem, some updates can be removed. To see if an update can be removed, look under Windows Update, click Installed Updates in the left window. This will take you to Control Panel, Programs. You will be able to see the installed updates.

Those which are not security updates and can be uninstalled will give you the option to uninstall. The page only lists updates that can be uninstalled. To see all updates that have been installed whether they are removable or not go to Windows Update and click View Update History.

Defragmenting Disks

When your system is a new system it is really fast and the computers processor has plenty of RAM, and when it runs out it has nice speedy hard drive space to act a virtual memory. What can happen if you don't maintain your hard disk?

What is fragmentation anyway?

When you first get your computer there is plenty of space to put your files anywhere and in a nice, easy to find space all together on the hard drive. But as you go along, the drive starts having a hard time trying to find enough space in between the little files it's placed for the bigger ones it is now placing on the drive. So the operating system starts splitting up the files and placing them all over the hard drive in pieces. After a while there are so many split up files that it slows the PC down looking for the files so it can piece them all back together and show you that nice 200MB PDF you want to see so bad. It doesn't seem like much until you know that on an NTFS volume larger than 2 GB in size, the cluster size is 4 KB. So if you have 400MB movie it is over 100,000 fragmented pieces.

After a while hard disk performance becomes a bottleneck and everyday your operation of the PC starts to slow things down. It starts with being noticed when you play movies, video clips, and perform DVD-burning. A little while longer your hard drive becomes slow even opening a small Word document or going to the Internet.

That is where Windows Defragmenter becomes your friend. I recommend you defrag your hard disks weekly. I you do, it should only take about 10 to 20 minutes and your hard drive will always stay healthy in terms of fragmentation. The longer you wait, the longer it takes to defragment the hard disks. I was called to a customer that had slowness at a cement plant recently. The PC was 4 years old and probably has never been defragmented. It took the PC about 2 days to perform this simple routine. Imagine all the frustration and lost productivity she had because of the lack of knowledge of this small simple process.

Windows Defragmenter has been in every version of Windows. In Windows 7 it is improved. Unlike previous versions Disk Defragmenter allows you to configure it to run as a low-priority background task once a week. If you set it run in the middle of the night, unless you are a night owl, you can set it and forget it. Let it run on its own.

Figure 7.3 shows Windows Defragmenter by going to Start, All Programs, Accessories, System Tools, and the Disk Defragmenter.

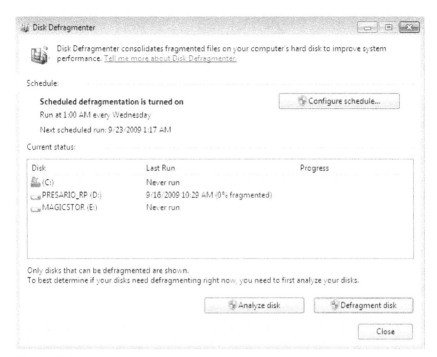

Figure 7.3

To configure Windows Disk Defragmenter to run on its own click the, "Configure Schedule...", button and the scheduler window will appear as shown in Figure 7.4.

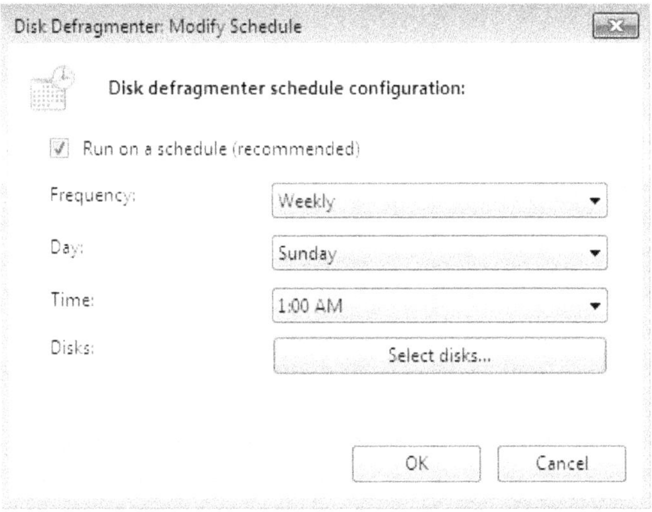

Figure 7.4

Pick a day of the week, the time and then select the disk you would like this to run on as shown in Figure 7.5.

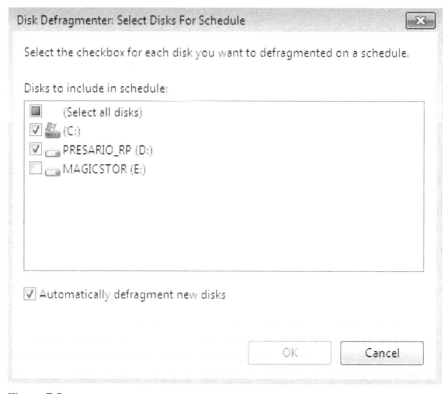

Figure 7.5

Selecting the, "Automatically defragment new disks" will auto add any drives which are connected whether they are large USB or even thumb drives. So it truly is a set it and forget it utility.

Running Disk Defragmenter

Disk Defragmenter allows you to run additional options from the command line. To use disk defragmenter from the command line, type "cmd" at the Windows Programs Bar Search for Files and Programs box. This brings up a Command Prompt window. Next type defrag followed by the drive letter. For instance if you wanted to defrag drive c: you would type "defrag d:" followed by any options you want. To see all of Windows Defragmenters options, type defrag /? at the command prompt.

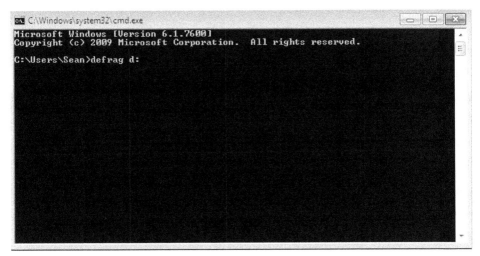

Let's take a look at the options available for the defrag command:

−c   This option defragments all volumes on the computer; use this switch without specifying a specific drive letter or mount point.

−a   This option analyzes the specified volume and displays a summary of the analysis report.

-f   This option consolidates the free space on the specified volume, reducing the chance that large new files will be fragmented.

/r   This option defragments multiple volumes in parallel. If your volumes are on physically separate disks, you might save a bit of time by using this switch.

-v   This option displays complete (verbose) reports. When it used in combination with −a, this switch displays only the analysis report. When used alone, it displays both the analysis and defragmentation reports.

−w   This option performs a full defragmentation by consolidating all file fragments, regardless of size.

–b   This option defragments only boot files and applications while leaving the rest of the drive undisturbed.

Note: *There is third party defragmenting software that can be used when Windows Defrag is not enough.*

Alert: *The Disk Defragmenter run from the command prompt does not provide any progress bar. Just a blinking cursor is shown. You can click the Command Prompt window and press CTRL+C to stop the process..*

Windows Check Disk (CHKDSK) and (CHKNTFS)

Along with Defragmenting, your hard disk can get errors as well. If these errors are not me operating system it will continue to place data on these areas. If the data is from these bad areas are not moved from these bad areas of the disk your computer can become unstable and even have what we call a crash. Windows Check Disk can automatically fix disk or file system errors or just look for them and report it to you. It comes in two flavors. One for NTFS drives called chkntfs and one for FAT and FAT32 drives called chkdsk. Let's take a look at both in the next two sections.

CHKDSK

Technically speaking, chkdsk is a DOS utility as shown in Figure 7.6 with the different syntaxes and options you can use. It also has a nice GUI with basic controls that you can run by right clicking a drive letter in Computer, right click the drive letter you want to scan, choose Properties, Error-checking, and then Check Now as shown in Figure 7.7 and 7.8.

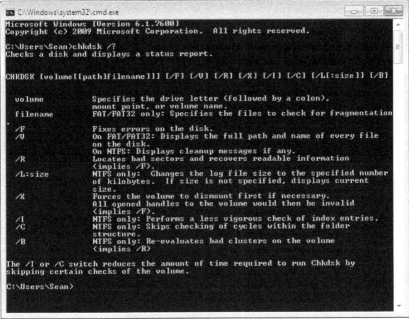

Figure 7.6

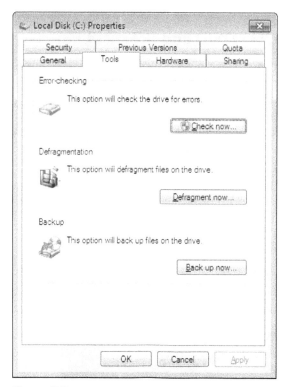

Figure 7.7

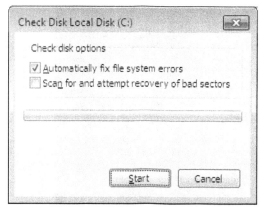

Figure 7.8

By default you have the "Automatically fix file system errors", which is the equivalent of running the chkdsk command in DOS with the /F syntax.

If you check the "Scan For And Attempt Recovery Of Bad Sectors an exhaustive check of the entire disk to find bad sectors and recover readable information stored in those defective location will be run on the hard disk. (Usually requiring a reboot to perform this feature on the next start up.) This option is the equivalent of running the chkdsk command in ODS with the /R syntax.

> **Note:** *Unchecking both boxes simply gives you a report of file system errors without making any changes or error corrections and is the only option which usually does not require a reboot to perform.*

When a reboot is required for the disk checking, the disk check occurs at the beginning of the startup sequence. When your computer starts, a Windows screen notifying you that it's about to perform a scheduled disk check. If you want to delay this check, you have 10 seconds to cancel the operation by pressing the space bar and boot normally in to Windows 7.

If you allow the check to continue, after Check Disk is completed you will get an on screen report of the findings. If the check finds that there are no errors, you see a Disk Check Complete dialog box.

> **Note:** *If Check Disk finds any errors, it puts an entry message in the System Event Log and displays a dialog box listing the errors it found and the repairs it made.*

These are the typical uses of chkdsk for a user. There are other options a shown in 7.6 which are identical in chkntfs and we will explain those further in the next section.

CHKNTFS

Check disk has its own utility errors for drives formatted with NTFS called chkntfs. It is used to perform a thorough inspection for errors. Two versions of this utility are available—a graphical version that performs basic disk-checking functions, and a command-line version that provides a much more extensive set of customization options.

> **NOTE:** *Sometimes, Check Disk will run automatically after an abnormal shutdown. It is because a specific bit in the registry is set, which indicates that the file system is "dirty". This denotes to the operating systems that that possible data was not properly written to the disk when the system was shut down. NTFS volumes keep a journal of all disk activities and use this information to recover the file system in the event of an abnormal shutdown.*

With the chkntfs command there are several syntaxes as shown in Figure 7.9.

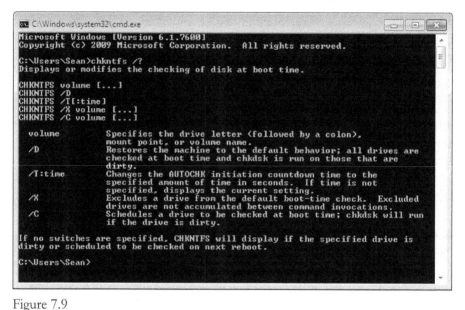

Figure 7.9

You can use any combination of the following switches at the end of the command line to modify the operation of chkntfs as shown below:

/F   This option attempts to fix any errors Chkdsk detects. The disk must be locked and may require a reboot to perform a dismount of the volume you want to check.

/V   This option work differently on different volume types. On FAT32 volumes, using this option displays the name of every file in every directory during the disk check. On NTFS volumes, this option displays only cleanup messages.

/R   This option identifies bad sectors and attempt to recover data from those sectors if possible. The disk must be locked.

/I   This option performs a simpler check of index entries reducing the amount of time required to complete the check only on NTFS volumes.

/C   This option skips the checking of cycles within the folder structure and reduces the amount of time required only on NTFS volumes.

/X   This option forces the volume to dismount only on NTFS volumes.

/L[:size]   This option adjusts the size of the NTFS transactions log only on NTFS volumes.

/B	This option reevaluates bad clusters only on NTFS volumes.
/P	This option performs an exhaustive check of the disk in the Windows Recovery Environment only on NTFS volumes.
/R	This option repairs bad spots found on the disk in the Windows Recovery Environment only on NTFS volumes.

Disk Cleanup

The Disk Cleanup utility is a very quick utility to clean up the temporary files and other items that can be cleaned safely to make space. You can start this by pressing the Start Bar (Round Windows logo), then All Programs, Accessories, System Tools, then Disk Cleanup, and the Disk Cleanup: Drive Selection will come up as shown in Figure 7.10.

Note: If you click any "low disk space" warning, the Disk Cleanup tool opens automatically.

Figure 7.10

Once you choose the drive letter it will scan your drive and calculate how much space the tool can free up in the different categories. As shown in Figure 7.11.

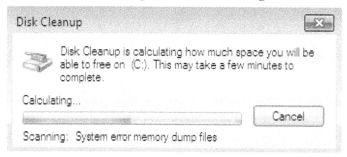

Figure 7.11

Obviously, I have a computer that is new as the total amount of free space I can free up is 19.5MB as shown in Figure 7.12. But typically if the utility has not been run in some time you can free up quite a bit of space.

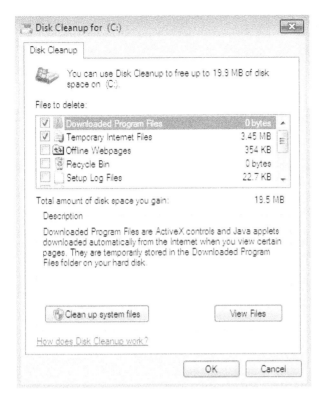

Figure 7.12

In Figure 7.13 I have scrolled down to show the additional options that I can choose from on the "Files to delete" box.

File 7.13

After all that I decided I needed to gain some space so I chose the first two options and I chose to delete the Thumbnails to give myself an extra 19.5MB of space. Once I selected those items and clicked OK, a confirmation box appeared as shown in Figure 7.14.

Figure 7.14

NOTE: *If you're not sure what's included in a file category, select it in the list and read the descriptive text. Also for some file categories, a View Files button is available; click that to open a folder containing the file category.*

If you did an upgrade to Windows 7 or an installation of Windows it placed your old operating systems files in a folder called Windows.old. You can reclaim a lot of disk space by deleting this folder or a majority of its contents.

Remote Assistance

Remote Assistance is a flexible tool that can be used in many different ways to support users in small to large enterprises. This section explains how to initiate Remote Assistance sessions from demonstrates how to use Remote Assistance in an enterprise Help Desk environment involving two common scenarios.

How to Create Remote Assistance Sessions

Remote Assistance sessions can be initiated either from the end user Graphic User Interface (GUI) or from a command line.

Initiating Remote Assistance from the GUI

1. Click Start Bar, then All Programs, click Maintenance, and then click Windows Remote Assistance. This launches the Windows Remote Assistance screen as shown in Figure 7.15.

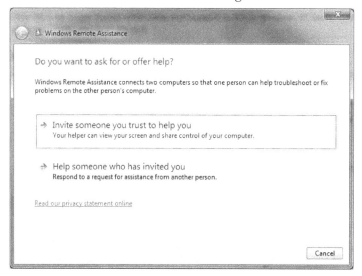

Figure 7.15

> **Note:** *you can also click Start Bar and type **assist** in the Start menu search box.*

2. You Remote Assistance to get help from someone by clicking the Invite Someone You Trust to Help You as shown in Figure 7.15.

> **Note:** *You can also click on "Who Has Invited You" option, which displays the Choose A Way to Connect to the Other Person's Computer. We will continue with the first option.*

3. Accept the Remote an invitation as a file from someone or offer Remote Assistance to someone by clicking the Help Someone

The following options are available:

Save This Invitation To A File-Selecting this option allows you to save your Remote Assistance invitation file to a folder. This folder can be location on your computer or an available network Share.

Use E-mail To Send An Invitation-Selecting this option launches your default e-mail client. A message is then created with an attached the invitation file.

Use Easy Connect-Selecting this option creates and publishes your Remote Assistance invitation file using and displays a 12-character password which you must communicate to whoever is helping you as shown below in Figure 7.16.

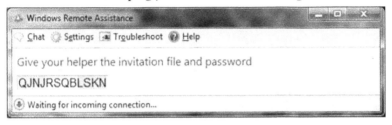

Figure 7.16

The other side must enter the password as shown below in Figure 7.17.

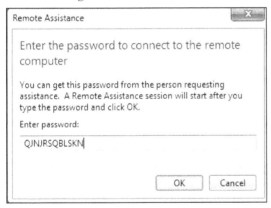

Figure 7.17

Sidebar: Record Problems

The Problem Steps Recorder (PSR) is a great new feature that helps in troubleshooting a system). At times, Remote Assistance may not be possible. Type **psr** in the Start Bar Search, it will launch the recorder as shown in Figure 7.18.

Figure 7.18

PowerShell

The Widows PowerShell is a feature for I.T.Pros to do common changes and support as shown in Figure 7.19.

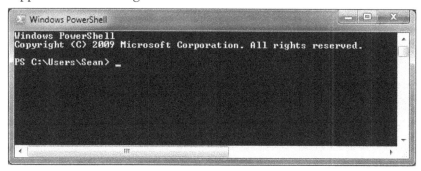

Figure 7.19

There are too many options to cover here in this book, but you should get to know the different option. Open the Start Bar and on the "Search programs and files" type: **PowerShell**.

System Configuration Tool

Like in previous versions of Windows there you can type in MSCONFIG at the "Search for Programs and Files" on the Start Bar and you get the System Configuration tool which you can use to identify problems that might prevent Windows from starting correctly.

This tool allows you to start Windows with common services and startup programs turned off or on. You can also experiment or troubleshoot by turning services on one at a time to help identify which services or boot line is causing a problem and help up you isolate problems.

In Figure 7.20 we see the System Configuration tool and all of its tabs.

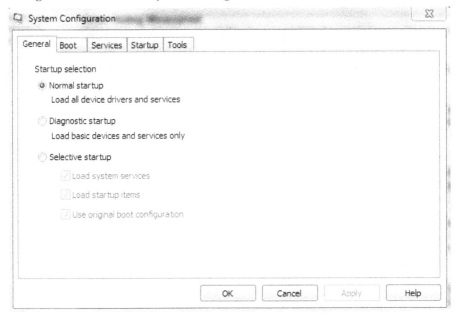

Figure 7.20

Let's take a look at each of the tabs pictured in Figure 7.20 one at a time.

General Tab

The General tab lists choices for startup configuration modes which are as follows:

Normal startup-This option starts Windows as it should always start in its ready state and properly working.

Diagnostic startup-This option starts Windows with the very basic services and drivers only.

Selective startup-This option starts Windows with basic services and drivers along with other services or startup programs that you select.

Boot Tab

This is a very important tab as seen in Figure 7.21, and shows configuration options for the operating system, advanced debugging settings, allows you to use more than one processor at boot, and limit the amount of ram that can be used.

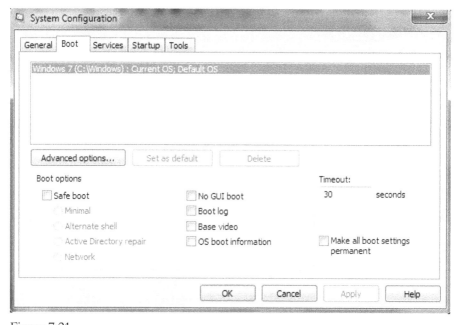

Figure 7.21

Let's look at these setting which including:

Safe boot(Minimal)-This startup option opens the Windows graphical user interface in safe mode loading only critical system drivers and services. Networking is disabled.

Safe boot(Alternate shell)- This startup option opens the Windows command prompt in safe mode. Again only running only critical system drivers and services. Networking and the graphical user interface are disabled.

Safe boot(Active Directory repair)-This startup option opens the Windows graphical user interface in safe mode loading only critical system drivers, services, and Active Directory.

Safe boot(Network)-This startup option opens the Windows graphical user interface in safe mode running only critical system drivers and services. Networking is enabled however.

No GUI boot-This startup option does not display the Windows Welcome screen at startup.

Boot log-This startup option stores all information from the startup process in the file %SystemRoot%Ntbtlog.txt on the hard drive.

Base video-This startup option opens the Windows graphical user interface in minimal VGA mode, using only standard VGA drivers.

OS boot information-This startup option Shows driver names as drivers are being loaded during the startup process.

Make all boot settings permanent-This startup option does not allow for tracking changes made in System Configuration. Options that are chosen can be changed manually in the System Configuration. If you choose this option you can't roll back your changes by selecting Normal startup on the General tab in the previous section.

Advanced Options Button

By pressing the Advanced Options on the Boot Tab menu, you have access to some very powerful tools such as the following:

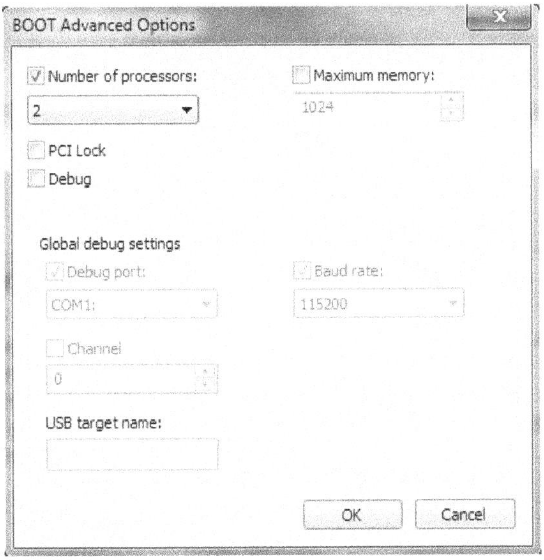

Figure 7.22

Number of processors-This option selects the number of processors to use on boot up on multiprocessor system as shown in Figure 7.22.

Maximum memory-This option specifies the maximum amount of physical memory used by the operating system. This is helpful when you want to simulate a low memory configuration. The value in the text box is megabytes (MB).

PCI Lock-This option stops Windows from reallocating I/O and IRQ resources on the PCI bus. The I/O and memory resources set by the BIOS are preserved.

Debug-This option enables kernel-mode debugging for device driver development.

Global debug settings are to troubleshoot a connection between the hosts a target computers using Serial, IEEE 1394, or USB 2.0 connectors. There are several option which are available:

Debug port-This option specifies you are using debugging usage of the serial port. The default port is COM 1.

Baud rate-This is an optional setting which specifies the baud rate to use when debugging the serial port. Possible baud rates are 9600, 19,200, 38,400, 57,600, or 115,200 bits per second (BPS). The default baud rate is 115,200 BPS.

Channel-This option specifies using 1394 as the debug connection type and specifies the channel number to use. The value for channel must be a decimal integer between 0 and 62, inclusive, and must match the channel number used by the host computer.

USB target name-This option specifies a string value to use when the debug type is USB. This string can be any value.

Services Tab

This tab shows a list of the services that start when the computer starts as shown in Figure 7.23. It also displays the current status of each service and states whether the service is "Running" or "Stopped".

You can also enable or disable individual services at startup which helps to troubleshoot services which might be causing startup problems.

Bu selecting "Hide all Microsoft services" you can see only third-party services installed on the computer. You can also clear the check box for a service to disable it the next time you start the computer.

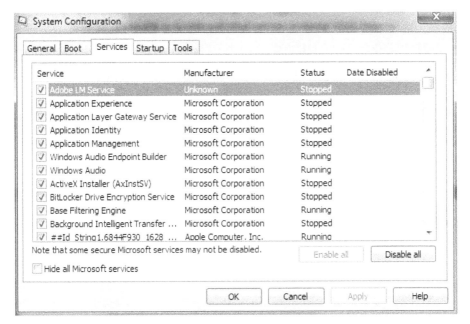

Figure 7.23

Note: *You must either choose Normal startup on the General tab or select the service's check box to allow non-critical services to run at startup.*

Warning: This tab actually allows you to disable critical startup services must run at startup. Disabling these might cause some programs to fail or result in system instability.

Startup Tab

This tab lists applications that run when the computer starts up as well as the path to the executable file, location of the registry key, or a shortcut that causes the application to run.

You can clear the check box for a startup item to disable it on your next startup.

Note: *You must either choose Normal startup on the General tab or select the service's check box to allow non-critical services to run at startup.*

Tools Tab

This tab provides a convenient list of diagnostic tools and other advanced tools that you can run. Such as the UAC, Action Center, Performance Monitor, and more.

Chapter 8 - Windows Backup

Many people don't see the value of using the backup utility until their hard disk crashes or the passenger side window in their car is on the ground and their laptop bag is missing. Almost everyone has work, personal pictures, or even music that they would miss if their computer or laptop was gone. People seem to understand backing up servers but backing up their PC's just does not occur to them. It almost takes a catastrophic loss of their data to start backing it up. By then it is too late.

In this section we will look at the following:

- How to configure a backup
- How create a disk image
- How to back up the Registry
- How to create a recovery disc

Configuring a Backup

When you save things to your laptop, install software on your PC or make changes to your computer, it brings a certain level of risk. Timely, complete, and functional backups allow you to minimize that risk. The Backup and Restore utility in Windows 7 allows you to backup and restore either your selected files all the files on the operating system.

There are several ways to Backup and Restore Center. One of the easiest is to press the Start button and type backup, then select Backup and Restore as shown in Figure 8.1.

Figure 8.1

You can also open up the Control Panel and select System and Security and select Backup and Restore as shown in Figure 8.2.

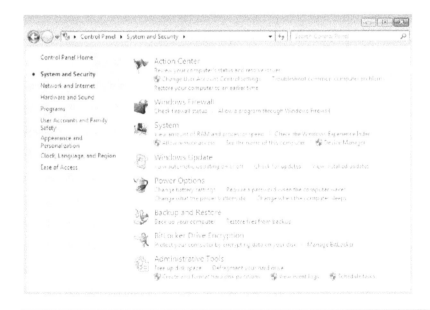

Figure 8.2

After you click on the Backup and Restore button you will see the Backup utility screen shown in Figure 8.3.

Figure 8.3

To backup your files, first click the "Set up backup..." button.

Windows will now prepare your system for backup and present you with a list of all the media it has found to perform a backup as shown below in Figure 8.4. You will notice that I have selected the FreeAgent USB drive using drive E:.

> **NOTE:** *To restore a file form a backup, launch Backup and Restore and click Restore Files. Locate the backup media your files are stored on and follow the instructions to get your previously backed up files back.*

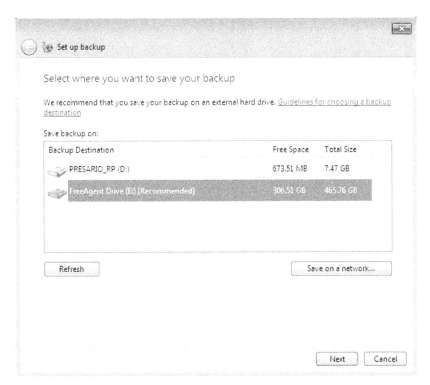

Figure 8.4

NOTE: *If you have a CD ROM/DVD Writer installed you will have the option to write the backup to that location as well. There is no additional software needed.*

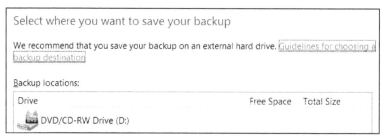

Select where you want to save your backup

We recommend that you save your backup on an external hard drive. Guidelines for choosing a backup destination

Backup locations:

Drive	Free Space	Total Size
DVD/CD-RW Drive (D:)		

I tend to know what I want to back up so I choose, "Let me choose" as shown in Figure 8.5. But if you are unsure or have very little administration experience with backing up data with one or previous versions of Windows, I would select the first option which allows Windows to decide what should be backed up.

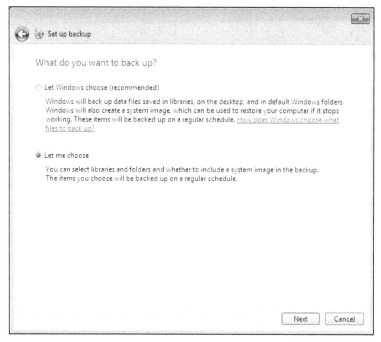

Set up backup

What do you want to back up?

○ Let Windows choose (recommended)

Windows will back up data files saved in libraries, on the desktop, and in default Windows folders. Windows will also create a system image, which can be used to restore your computer if it stops working. These items will be backed up on a regular schedule. How does Windows choose what files to back up?

● Let me choose

You can select libraries and folders and whether to include a system image in the backup. The items you choose will be backed up on a regular schedule.

[Next] [Cancel]

Figure 8.5

The next screen that appears in Figure 8.6 allows you to choose what you would like to backup by placing a checkmark next to the item I want to backup.

Figure 8.6

After you click Next, there is just one last screen that appears to allow us to review all the settings we have selected as shown in Figure 8.7.

Figure 8.7

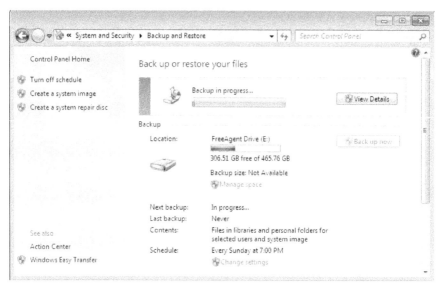

Figure 8.8

In Figure 8.8, you see that our backup is about five percent complete. This is a running progress bar. Also below the backup in progress status bar you see the drive you are backing your data up to and the amount of free space still available. It is a blue bar unless the space available on the drive becomes less than ten percent and then it will turn red.

When the backup is running you will see a small clock on the flag in to the Superbar as shown below in Figure 8.9.

Figure 8.9

When your backup is completed you can go back and edit the settings to configure the frequency of your backup and make it an automated process. You can set how often, the day, and the time as shown below in Figure 8.10. I do recommend however that if you rely on this process to work, check to make sure the backup has run on a regular basis. I would also do a test restore which to make sure that what you are backing up is restorable.

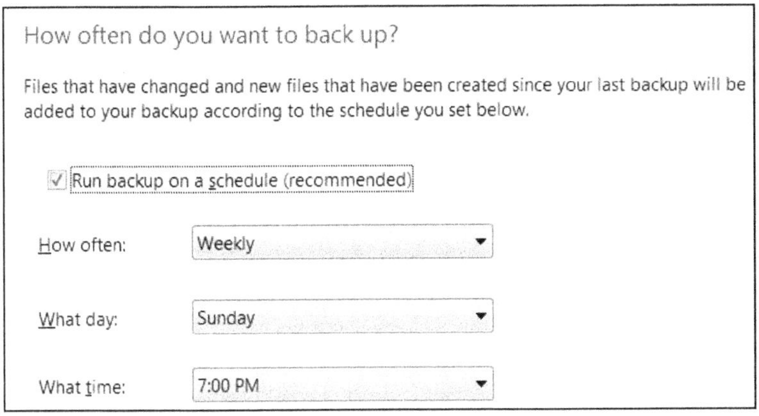

How often do you want to back up?

Files that have changed and new files that have been created since your last backup will be added to your backup according to the schedule you set below.

☑ Run backup on a schedule (recommended)

How often: Weekly ▼

What day: Sunday ▼

What time: 7:00 PM ▼

Figure 8.10

Create System Image

A system image is one of the fastest ways to restore your hard disk. This is different than a backup which you select the data you want to backup. If you do a restore it is done on an operating system that is functioning well enough to do the restore. A system images an exact copy of the disk or partition at the time the image was made.

It is also an excellent way of installing the same configuration and software on multiple PC's. You can install the operating system and all the software on one PC or laptop, create an image and then you can copy that image to all the other new PC's or laptops. From a DVD it takes about 10-20 minutes to install the PC's.

> **NOTE:** *You should not activate Windows on the PC or laptop you are creating the image from. That way you can activate the Windows key that came with each individual PC or laptop.*

To create an image, first on the Backup and Restore menu in the Control Panel you will see the "Create a system image" link on the left as shown in Figure 8.11.

Figure 8.11

Once you click on the link in Figure 8.10, you will get a screen that allows you to choose where you would like the image to be stored. You will see that I have a 300GB FreeAgent USB drive attached which I have chosen to place the system image on this drive. But along with attached drives, you have the option to place it on DVD or to a network location as well as shown in Figure 8.12.

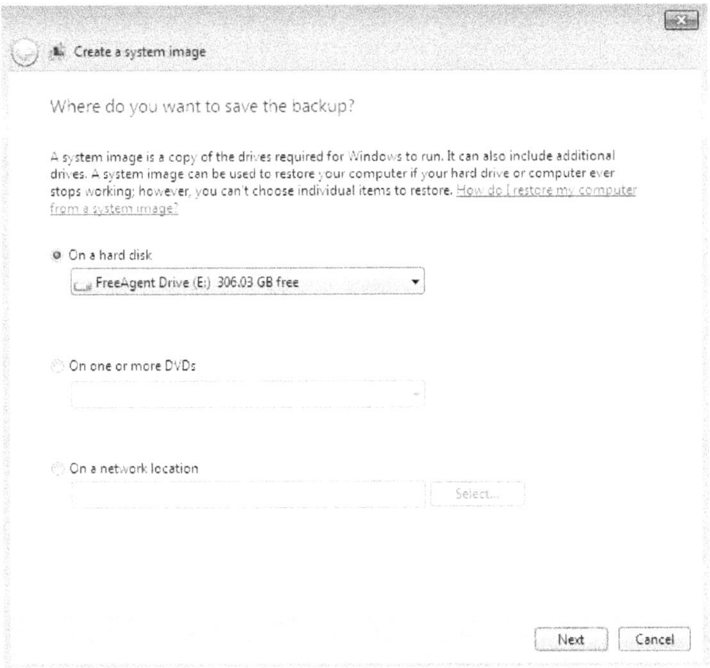

Figure 8.12

After you have selected a media location that has enough space for the image, Windows 7 will give you a confirmation screen before starting as shown in Figure 8.13. It will also display the drive letters of the drives you will be creating an image of.

Figure 8.13

The image will start by clicking the Start Backup button as shown in Figure 8.14.

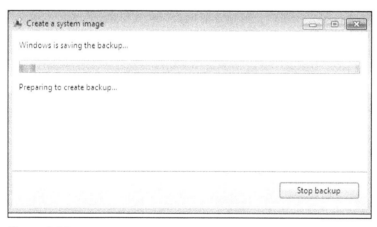

Figure 8.14

Backing up the Registry

Occasionally, when troubleshooting or making changes to the operating system, you will have to make changes to the registry and it might become corrupt. Some troubleshooting steps require you to change values in your registry. If you make a mistake and don't correct it, you may find your computer no longer functions as it did before. To protect yourself from any mistakes or other system problems, you need to backup your registry.

To backup the registry, first open the registry by going to the Start button and then type regedit as shown in Figure 8.15.

Figure 8.15

Then left click Computer in the left side pane as shown in Figure 8.16.

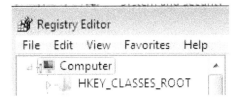

Figure 8.16

Next, choose File and then Export. A window similar to the one in Figure 8.17 will appear. Choose the location you want to save the file and then press Save.

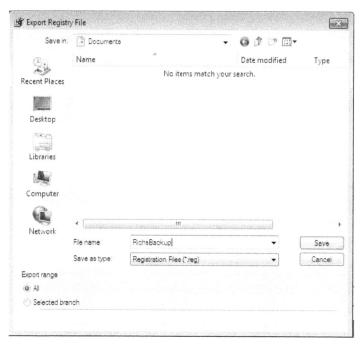

Figure 8.17

NOTE: *To restore the registry follow the same instructions but choose Import instead of Export.*

Create a System Recovery Disc

If Windows 7 becomes corrupt you can avoid a full installation of the operating system by having a System Recovery Disc. You can use this disc to attempt a repair at boot up. The system recovery disc cannot be used to install or reinstall Windows, but it can be used to fix common problems that prevent Windows from booting.

To create a system recovery disc, do the following. First, open the Backup and Restore utility and then click the link called, "Create a system repair disc". As shown in Figure 8.18.

Figure 8.18

After you click on the link, the screen shown in Figure 8.19 will appear and allow you to select your DVD drive. Once you have selected the drive, click Create disc.

Figure 8.19

NOTE: *You will need a blank writable DVD to make the disc.*

Chapter 9 – Other New Windows 7 Features

Windows 7 is packed with a whole host of new features. In this chapter, we'll take a look at some of these new features which we have not covered already in this book. We will look at how they can help you work more efficiently on your computer. This is not an exhaustive break down of each feature; but it will bring an awareness of what Windows 7 has to offer.

In this chapter we will cover:

- Federated Search
- Snip Tool
- Sticky Notes
- Personal Character Edition
- Device Stage
- ReadyBoost
- Branch Cache
- Internet Explorer

Federated Search

The new Federated Search tool is used to search beyond the scope of your local PC hard drives for relevant content. It is based on Open Search and RSS to allow you to search remote repositories. You can use third party search connectors or create your own connectors, which is very easy because of the standard format used by Open Search.

There are already many search connectors available for you to download from:

- Bing
- Deviant Art Search
- Flickr Search Connector
- Google Blogs Search Connector
- Google News Search Connector
- Microsoft Windows Live Search Connector
- MSN Search
- Twitter Search Connector
- YouTube Search Connector

As more sites add support for OpenSearch, expect to see more search connectors emerging for Windows 7. I am sure with the ease of creating a search connector the list of available Federated Search tools will be as long as this book is.

> **Sidebar:** What is Open Search?
>
> OpenSearch is a collection of simple formats for the sharing of search results. You can use OpenSearch formats to help people discover relevant content search results across the web. It's like having your own personal search engine, but others can create search tools to search their own personal or corporate libraries.
>
> The Internet is a big place, and search engines only crawl the surface of the web and only find a small fraction of the great content that is out there. Moreover, some of the richest and most interesting content cannot even be crawled and indexed by one search engine.

OpenSearch also helps search engines and search clients communicate by introducing a common set of formats to perform search requests and syndicate search results.

You might be surprised that OpenSearch was created by A9.com, which ix an Amazon.com company, and the OpenSearch format is now in use by hundreds of search engines and search applications on the Internet.

I went ahead and created a Search Connector for Microsoft's Bing.com search engine. In Appendix C of this book, you can see the steps I used, links to learn how to do it yourself and you can copy my code until your heart is content. It took me about three hours to create the code for which I saved as Bing.osdx on the desktop as shown in Figure 9.1.

Figure 9.1

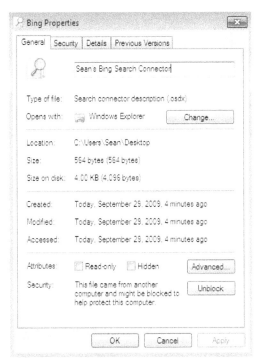

If I right click on the file you will see the properties in Figure 9.2.

Figure 9.2

You see in Figure 9.1, I have also clicked on the icon for the Bing search connector I created and it asks me if it is Ok to install. I clicked the Add button and it installs in only a few seconds. I now have a new search connector under favorites in my Libraries as shown below in Figure 9.3.

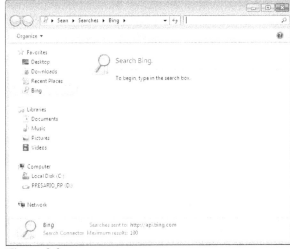

Figure 9.3

Snip Tool

One of the coolest little additions to Windows Vista and carried over to Windows 7 is the Snipping Tool. This tool allows you to move your mouse and take a picture of as large of a square of your screen as you would like and make it in to a picture. It then can be saved as a picture or copied to a document. Down below you will see that I have several Sticky Notes on my desktop. If I did a Shift+Print Screen, I would get the entire screen. But the Snipping Tool allows me to highlight only the area I want to copy as shown in Figure 9.4. Here I have only copied the Sticky notes and not the entire desktop screen. I can also write or draw a picture on the already captured picture or erase parts that I don't want as well. A very fun little tool.

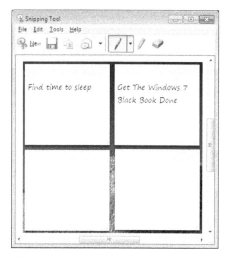

Figure 9.4

Sticky Notes

This is another fun little tool included with Windows 7. We are all familiar with the Post It notes we have on our desks. Well Windows 7 makes them go digital. Put little reminders on your screen and even use it as your task list. If you want another Post It, click the "+" sign. They will continue across your screen as shown in Figure 9.5. If they run out of room they will overlap. If you are done with one, click the "X" and delete it. The cool thing is that if you shut off your computer, they will be back just like you left them on your desktop. The ones in Figure 9.6 have been on my desktop for weeks.

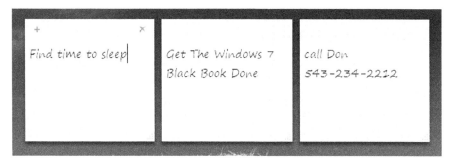

Figure 9.5

Figure 9.6

Personal Character Editor

Have you ever wanted to create your own font characters? Well here is your chance with the Personal Character Edition included in Windows 7 under Accessories. You can use this feature to create your own letters and font. Simply click on the boxes where you want to illuminate pixels as shown in Figure 9.7.

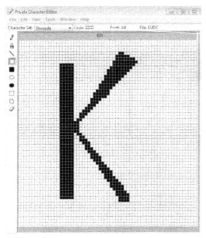

Figure 9.7

Jump Lists

Jump Lists are a new feature in Windows 7. Jump Lists don't just show shortcuts to files, they are items that you go to frequently. Once you have opened a document, music, or any other file, if you right click on the icon on the Superbar it will show the items you recently opened. If you hover over an item with your mouse and a pushpin will appear on the right of the line you're hovering over. Click the pushpin on the right and you will pin that on the Jump List. This means that item will always be there when you restart Windows or log off and then back on. (You can click again to unpin as well.)

Let's take a look at an example. In Figure 9.8 you see the documents I have recently opened. I am working on the Windows 7 Black Book and I have been frequently opening it.

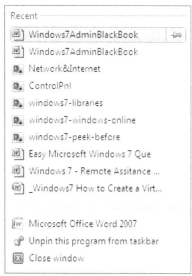

Figure 9.8

Since I have just started on the book I need to open it a lot and I don't want to search the hard drive for my document and waste time. So I am going to click on the pushpin to the right as shown in Figure 9.9. From here on regardless of how many times I log off and log on or open other documents, the items I push a pushpin on will always be there.

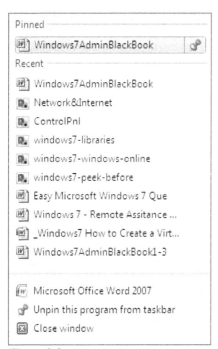

Figure 9.9

You can also pin applications to the Start Bar and also pin documents to those application as shown below in Figure 9.10.

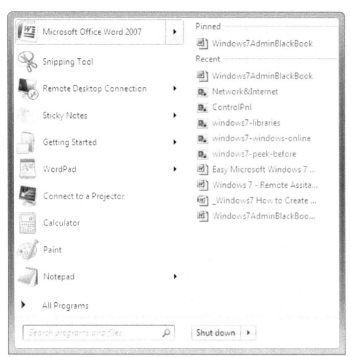

Figure 9.10

ReadyBoost

Remember when your old computer got slow because there was not enough RAM? You had to go run to the computer store and find these little RAM sticks that gave you more RAM and made your PC faster. Not anymore! Now you can use a thumb drive? What? No kidding. I increased the Physical Memory of the Windows 7 PC I am using by 2GB by using a blank solid state thumb drive and ReadyBoost.

If you plug a ReadyBoost-compatible storage device into your computer, the AutoPlay dialog box offers you the option to install ReadyBoost.

Once you select the option to install ReadyBoost, Windows shows you how much space you should use on the drive with a recommendation for optimal performance as shown in Figure 9.11.

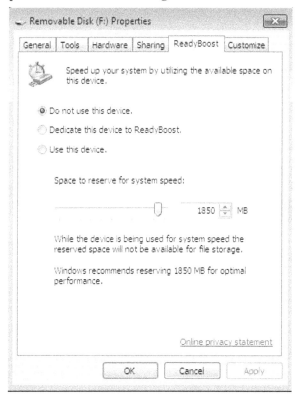

Figure 9.11

Next, choose the second or third options to use the device for ReadyBoost. If you will be using the device for ReadyBoost only, you can choose the second option as shown in Figure 9.12 and use all the available space on the drive. If you choose the last option you can use the scroll bar to choose how much space to dedicate to physical memory.

Figure 9.12

It's really easy to use Windows ReadyBoost. And if the ReadyBoost device is not present it will not harm the operation of the Windows operating system. You can use almost any removable memory device such as a USB flash drive or a secure digital (SD) memory card.

ReadyBoost was originally introduced in Windows Vista but was a little known feature. There was a 4GB restriction in Windows Vista but that has been removed so larger flash drives can be used. The limit of one ReadyBoost device has also been removed which gives users the possibility to use multiple flash drives as additional caches in Windows 7. In Figure 9.12 you see the new ReadyBoost drive shown as Disk1 on the Computer Managements, Disk Management option.

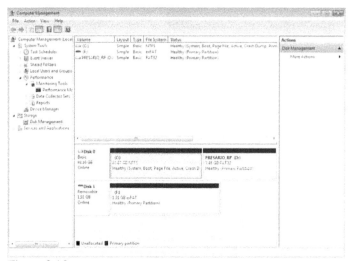

Figure 9.12

Branch Cache

Windows BranchCache is included in Windows Server 2008 R2 and Windows 7. BranchCache is a new feature and is not based on the ISA server as many people believe.

Basically this feature allows a client to only read content from a peer (or hosted cache server) which matches the content hashes the client retrieved from the original content server.

Meaning that the host server will download content once for the original requesting client and then cache a copy of the same material.

> **Alert:** *It appears that the BranchCache service takes over port 80 which interferes with using Apache on a workstation.*

Configure Branch Cache Server

BranchCache, focused mainly on optimizing your WAN bandwidth using special cache options available only in Windows Server 2008 R2. BranchCache works in scenarios with branch offices where clients interact and request files from a central location such as a headquarters.

BranchCache is a simple idea that caches the content downloaded from the central location using a server or other branch clients. Every time that a second client tries to download the content, the request is directly handled within the branch office optimizing the WAN link and downloading time.

There are no complex configurations and you can even use an option that does not include a server. There are two types of BranchCache deployment options: Distributed Cache (no server) and Hosted Cache Mode (Windows Server 2008 R2 server).

> **Alert:** *Distributed Cache environment will only work with Windows Server 2008 R2 and Windows 7 clients.*

To configure the Windows 2008 R2 file server to be a BranchCache server, select the Add Features Wizard in the Server Manager and select BranchCache as shown in Figure 9.13.

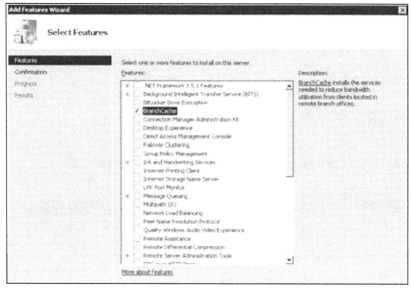

Figure 9.13

File Services role and the service must be selected to handle BranchCache for remote files as shown in Figure 9.14.

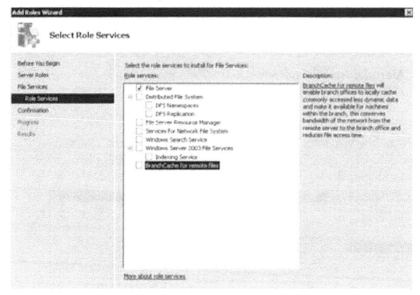

Figure 9.14

You must now configure Group Policy (GPO) to enable BranchCache.

> **NOTE:** *Active Directory is recommended but not a requirement for BranchCache.*

You can use an Active Directory or local policy to apply to this server. The GPO can be located in the Computer Configuration, Policies, Administrative Templates, Network, Lanman Server, and Hash Publication for BranchCache as shown in Figure 9.15.

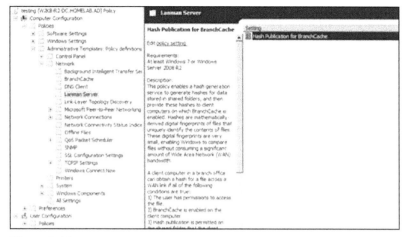

Figure 9.15

When you click on the, "Hash Publication for BranchCache" option you will get the screen in Figure 9.16 which allows you to enable BranchCache. Click on Enable and select, "Allow hash publication for all file servers."

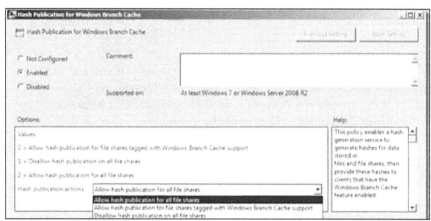

Figure 9.16

BranchCache Client Configuration

On the Windows 7 Client it is pretty easy to configure as well. First you need to configure the GPO by editing the settings in the MMC. You do this by going to Computer Configuration, Policies, Administrative Templates, Network, Turn on BranchCache, and then enable the option as shown in Figure 9.17.

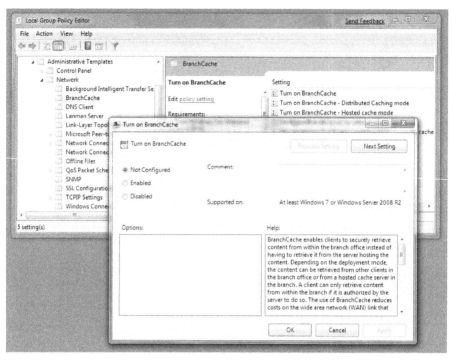

Figure 9.17

Also in Figure 9.17 you need to set several other options. If you are using Distributed Cache, enable "Turn on BranchCache – Distributed Caching Mode". Or if you are using hosted cache mode you will need to enable, "Turn on BranchCache" and select "Hosted Cache mode".

Optionally, you can also set other values using this set of GPOs, like latency values or setting a percentage of your disk space dedicated to this cache. Also you will need to ensure that you have configured the firewall inbound policies to allow BranchCache connections. 3. Configure the Cache Server

For more information you can go to:

http://www.microsoft.com/downloads/details.aspx?displaylang=en&FamilyID=a9a1ed8a-71ab-468e-a7e0-470fd46e46b3

Internet Explorer 8

Internet Explorer 8 is Microsoft's latest web browser, which comes packed with many new features. Below is an explanation of how to get IE8 up and running and use some of the new features.

Let's take a look at a few new features including Quick Tabs and In Private viewing features.

Quick Tabs

The Quick Tabs button is the 4 little boxes with the down arrow next to the left of the tabs. They show you all currently open tabs at a glance to help you select the page you need. Each tab shows a scaled down window of the current website you are viewing as shown in Figure 9.18.

Figure 9.18

Improved Search

The search feature has been greatly improved, with smart suggestions and even an inline search as shown in Figure 9.19.

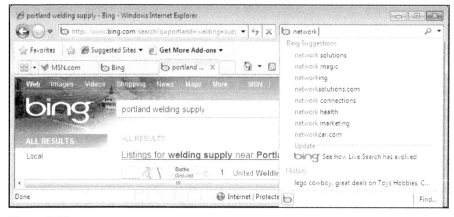

Figure 9.19

InPrivate Browsing

InPrivate Browsing helps prevent websites from and Internet Explorer from obtaining or storing data about your browsing sessions. This includes cookies, temporary Internet files, history, and Windows 7 Features other data. Toolbars and extensions are disabled by default when you use this feature.

To turn on this feature go to Safety and select InPrivate browsing as shown in Figure 9.20.

Note: *To turn off the feature repeat the same process.*

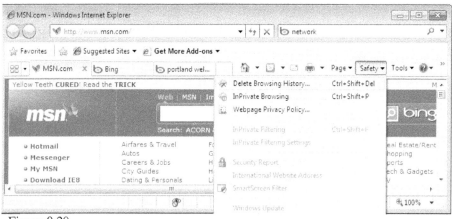

Figure 9.20

In Figure 9.21, you will notice the new InPrivate logo next to the address in the Address Toolbar on the browser.

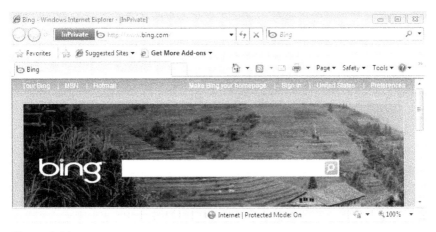

Figure 9.21

Chapter 10 – Devices and Printers

Windows 7 makes installing devices and printers about as easy as you can make it. Unlike with Windows XP when Windows Vista came out we had to wait for a lot of plug and play device and printer drivers. In Windows 7, all Vista 32 and 64 bit drivers are compatible. Notice in Figure 10.1, I have no printers installed except for the default Microsoft XPS Document writer. But in real like I have an HP OfficeJet 1300n and a Lexmark 7350. In this section we will walk through installing my HP OfficeJet 1300n. We will also look at changing the printer properties as well.

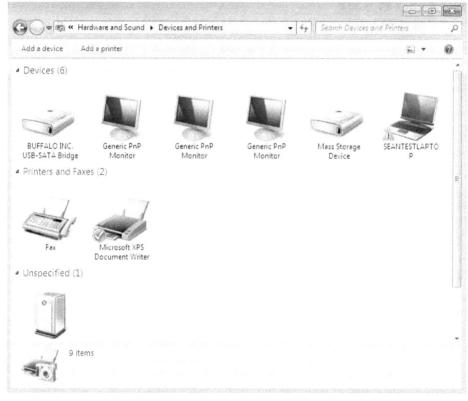

Figure 10.1

Installing a Printer or Device

First, I am going to go to Start, Control Panel, Hardware and Sound as shown in Figure 10.2 below.

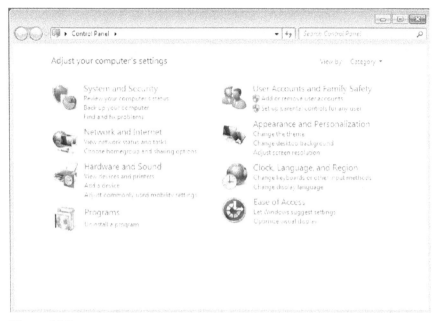

Figure 10.2

Next, unlike going to Printers like previous Windows versions I am going to choose add a device and I see the screen shown in Figure 10.3.

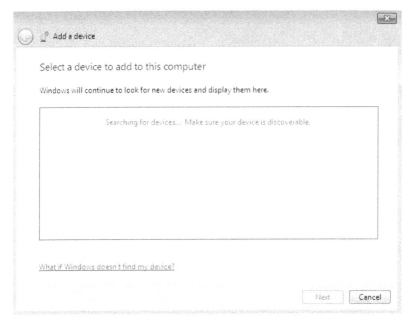

Figure 10.3

Next, I am simply going to plug in the printer and Windows should give you an acknowledgement as show in Figure 10.4. I am using printers that had drivers built in to Widows 7. If I bought a new printer or a device that did not have a driver that was built in, you would either need to download the Vista or Windows 7 driver from the Internet or install them from a CD or DVD. It is always safer to install the driver for the printer or the device before plugging the device in.

Figure 10.4

If the printer driver does not match a plug and play device you will see the window shown in Figure 10.5 to allow you to either select the printer or select, "Have Disk…" to install the driver if you have one.

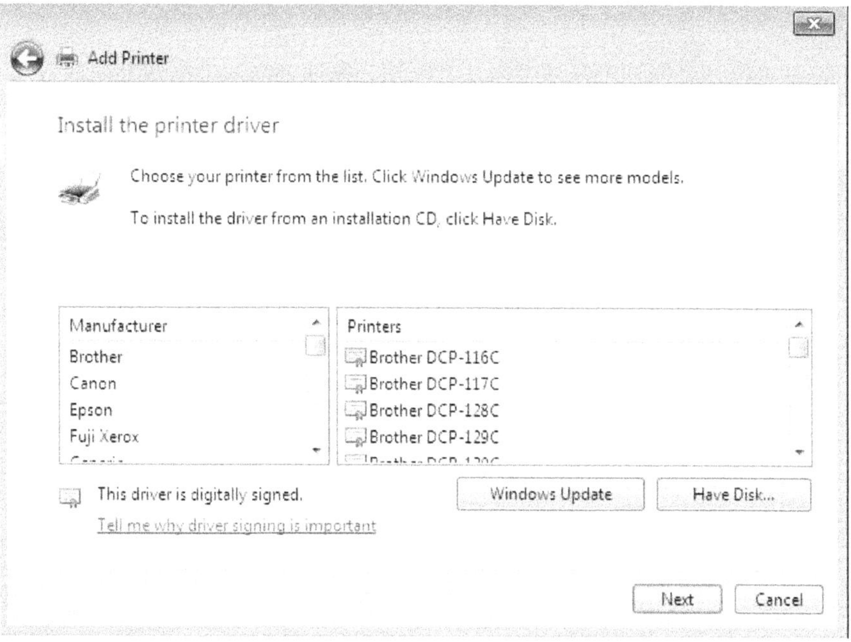

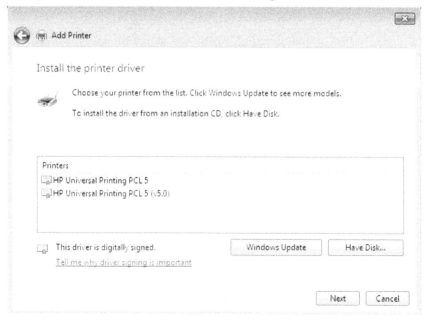

Figure 10.5

The printer I am installing already has a plug and play driver so I get a pop up asking me which driver to install as shown in Figure 10.6.

Figure 10.6

Next, I receive a screen to identify a name that I will use to identify this printer as shown in Figure 10.7.

Figure 10.7

When you enter a name and click Next. You will then see the following screen indicating the printer is installing in Figure 10.8.

Figure 10.8

The next screen you will see will indicate that you have installed the printer successfully and give you the option to print a test page as shown in Figure 10.9.

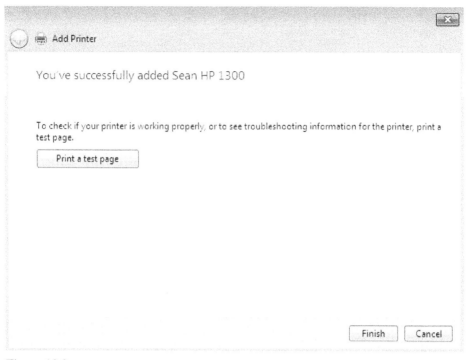

Figure 10.9

Printer Properties

Windows 7 allows device manufacturers to create their own properties pages as you can see from the Properties page shown below in Figure 10.10. This is a screenshot from my Lexmark 7350 printer.

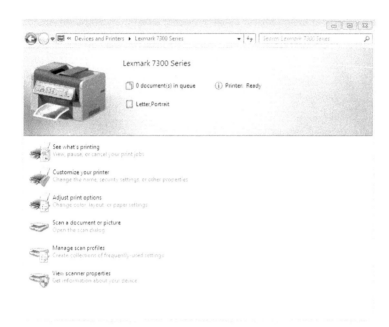

Figure 10.10

The screens that manufacturers can create are very graphical as shown on Figure 10.11.

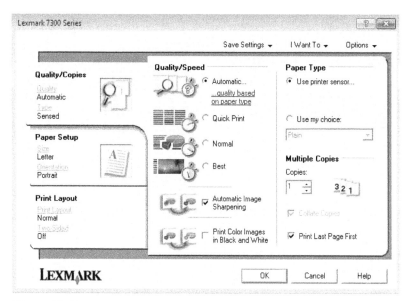

Figure 10.11

Now that we have seen the Properties for the Lexmark printer, let's take a look at the typical properties screen as shown in Figure 10.12 Printing Shortcuts tab.

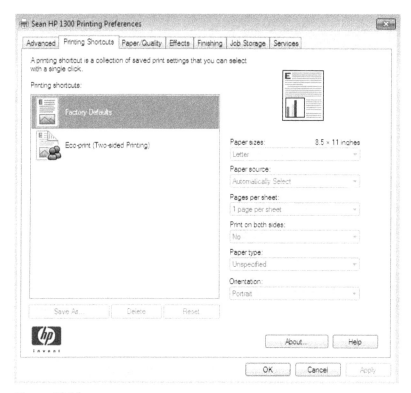

Figure 10.12

The General Tab is where you can identify the location of the printer, a description, or try a test print as shown below in Figure 10.13.

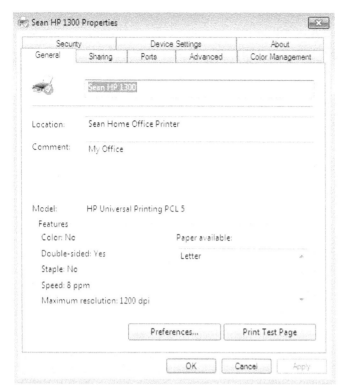

Figure 10.13

The rest of the tabs are pretty similar to those found in previous versions of Windows. For more information on each item please see:

http://windows.Microsoft.com/en-US/windows7/Choosing-print-options

NOTE: *If a printer is configured on an Active Directory domain controller and you add a Windows computer's account, the printer will be installed on the PC or laptop.*

Chapter 11 – Managing and Maintaining Windows 7 Workstations

Have you ever had to use a slow computer? Delayed responses, endless waits, very few things are more annoying. Fortunately, there are proven tools and techniques you can use to give your PC a big performance boost!

One of the first things I like to do when I am trying to determine why a PC is running so sluggishly is to Figure out which process or processes are using the most resources, then research the process(es) to determine if they can be linked to legitimate software or if they are potentially malware. To quickly ascertain which process(es) are utilizing the most resources you will need to...

1. Hold down Ctrl + Shift + Esc on your keyboard

2. Windows Task Manager Opens up > Click on the Performance Tab

3. Click on Resource Monitor

Resource Monitor

Resource Monitor first seen in Windows Vista, is a godsend to IT professionals who are attempting to quickly determine which processes are utilizing key computer resources as well as any current or potential bottlenecks the Workstation may have. The overview tab gives you a general idea of the current CPU, Disk, Network, and Memory usage and the processes utilizing the most resources in the category as shown in Figure 11.1. The additional tabs give you a more in-depth look at the specific resource. We will delve into each one as they are worth exploring.

>   **Note:** If you are unsure as to what a specific informational column is referring to, hold your mouse over the column to be given a description.

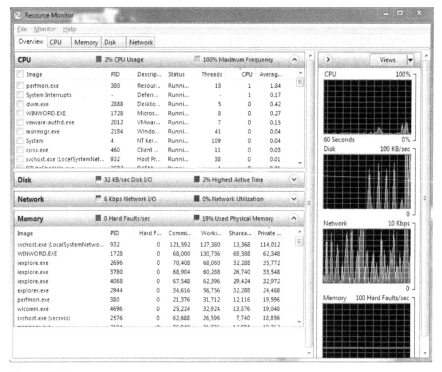

Figure 11.1

Resource Monitor - CPU Tab

The CPU Tab gives you a more detailed look at your CPU usage providing you the processes and services that are using the CPU the most, as well as showing you individual CPU's usage for multi-core, or multi-CPU systems. You can also select specific processes from the list to view the Modules and Handles Associated with the process. The process associated with Microsoft Word and it's relevant handles and modules is shown in Figure 11.2

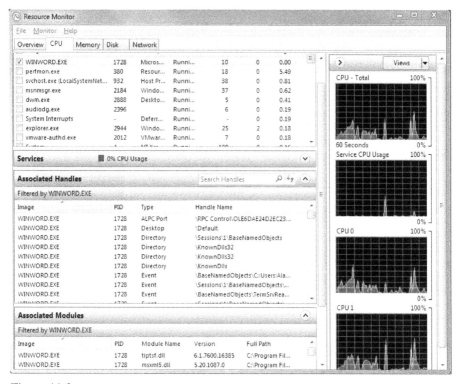

Figure 11.2

Resource Monitor - Memory Tab

The Memory Tab shows you the processes that are utilizing memory, a dynamic graph showing the current amount of Used Memory, Commit Charge, and Hard Faults/Sec, and a graphic showing you how Windows is using your memory and how much is available. This graphic, shown in Figure 11.3, can help you determine if you need to increase the amount of RAM in your system. Or perhaps add a Readyboost capable USB device (explained later in this chapter).

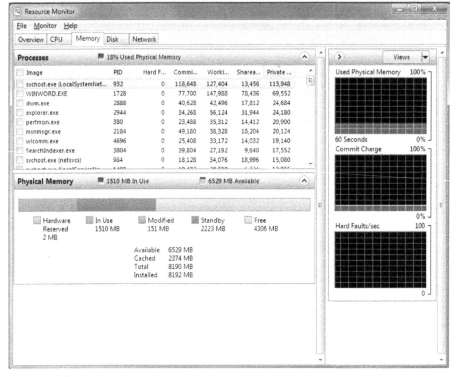

Figure 11.3

Resource Monitor - Disk Tab

The Disk Tab (Figure 11.4) shows you the processes utilizing your hard disks, the current queue length for the various disks connected to your computer, as well as the available space on the connected disks. The queue length can be used to determine if your system needs more RAM, or possibly a beefier disk array.

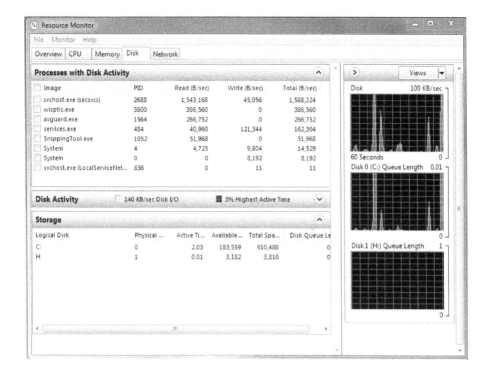

Figure 11.4

Resource Monitor - Network Tab

The Network Tab (Figure 11.5) shows you the current network activity for the various network adapters on your computer, the processes utilizing the network connections, and the list of current TCP connections and listening ports.

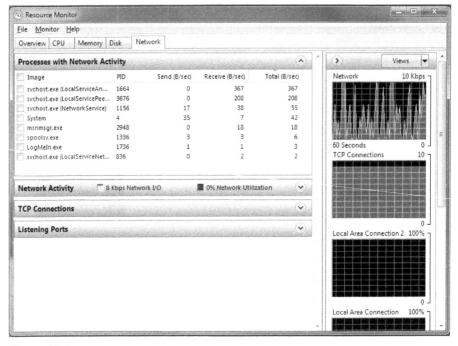

Figure 11.5

Performance Monitor

The performance monitor has been beefed up in Windows 7 to let you perform a variety of common IT tasks within. To access the performance monitor simply do the following:

1. Click the Windows Orb (Start Button)

2. In the Search Bar type in Perfmon.msc and press enter

   Note: For the most accurate performance data utilize Windows ability to monitor performance information of a computer from a remote workstation.

You can then use the Performance Monitor to do the following:

- View real time statistics of various system resources.

- Capture system resource usage over an extended period of time.

- Create a one time or ongoing schedule for resource data collection.

- Create Alerts and subsequent actions and tasks if system resources match specified thresholds.

- Create and Generate reports as well as view previously collected data
  Create and customize data collector sets and event trace sessions

View Real-Time Statistics or view previously gathered logs

The Performance Monitor tool within Performance Monitor can be used to view both real-time or logged datasets. The Performance Monitor tool can be accessed by expanding the monitoring tools section of Performance Monitor.

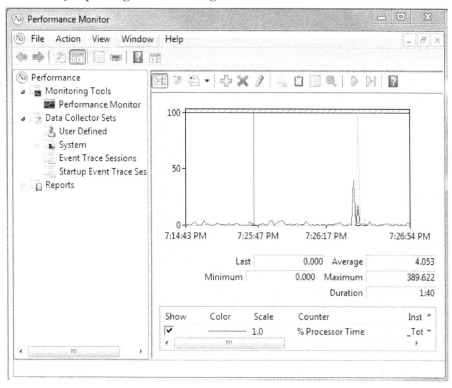

Figure 11.6

A variety of buttons are available for you to use as shown in Figure 11.6, but most options can be setup by choosing the properties icon or by pressing CTRL Q.

The Performance Monitor Properties Window presents you with 5 tabs...

> **General:** The general tab lets you change the overall performance monitor interface as well as what values you want presented in Reports and Histogram Data

> **Source:** The Source tab lets you choose whether you want to view Current Activity or previously collected log files or Databases. If you

select a log file or database the time range button becomes available allowing you to specify specific time ranges you'd like to view.

Data: The data tab lets you specify what counters are currently being collected or will be displayed out of a previous dataset as well as the color, line width, and scale of those counters. By default when you open a saved log file no counters are displayed. They must be manually added via the Data tab.

Graph: The Graph tab lets you specify how you want the data to be graphed as well as the minimum and maximum numbers you want to allow in the scale

Appearance: The appearance tab lets you specify the color of various object such as the Background, Text, and Grid as well as change the Font used or whether you want a border around the graph window.

Creating / Modifying / Using Data Collector Sets

The data collector sets section of Performance Monitor is used for the majority of Performance Monitor tasks including, creating alerts and subsequent tasks when thresholds are reached, creating reoccurring or one-time monitoring periods, and pulling system configuration information, Performance Counters, event trace data. Data collector sets can be grouped, added to log files, used as templates, and the data contained therein can be viewed in the Performance Monitor.

Creating Performance Counter Alerts

Wouldn't it be nice if you could create an alert on your servers and workstations that would warn you when specific system resources were impacting performance? The following steps outline the process of creating a alert.

1. In Performance Monitor Expand Data Collector Sets

2. Right Click the User Defined Section and Choose New > Data Collector Set

3. Give your collector set a name and choose the Create Manually option.

4. Choose Performance Counter

5. The next window asks you which performance counters you would like to monitor, click the Add button.

6. Choose the Counter(s) you would like to monitor and click the add button, click ok when done.

7. The counters you have chosen are listed in the performance counters pane.

8. For each counter type specify a limit, and determine whether you want the alert to proceed if the value is above or below the specified threshold as shown in Figure. Once you have set your desired limits click next.

9. Choose whether you want to run as another user or use the default (the System Account), and then decide whether you want to start the data collector set now, save and close, or edit the properties of the data collector set.

10. If you choose to edit the properties of the collector set you are presented with 6 tabs, General, Directory, Security, Schedule, Stop Condition, and Task, These tabs are the same for any custom collector set you create.

> **General:** The General Tab is used to describe the data collector set and give it select keywords. You can also use this tab to change the account being used to collect the specified data. Remember the account must have administrative capabilities, or be a member of the performance log users group.

> **Directory:** This tab is where you can specify what directory you want the data collector set information to be stored. If you wish the directory storing the data collector set data to be different then the data collector set directory, type in the desired name into the subdirectory field. The subdirectory name format field is where you specify the format for the auto generated directories. An example directory is shown at the bottom of the page.

> **Security:** Here you can specify users and groups that have various access levels to the user data set.

> **Schedule:** If you want to set a time frame when data in the set is collected, specify the schedule here.

> **Stop Condition:** Here you can specify various time or size stop conditions for the data collector set. You also have the option to stop when all collectors is finished, or restart the collector at the specified limits.

Task: Once the Data Collector Set stops you can specify a WMI command to run as well as task arguments for that command.

Editing Collectors within Data Collector Set

By selecting the Collector Set you can edit any of the collectors stored within. Alert collectors have 3 tabs available for you to edit.

Alerts: The Alerts tab is where you specify counters you want to monitor, as well as the interval period between taking sample data.

Alert Action: Here you specify if you want an entry to be put in the application log and/or another data collector set started.

Alert Task: Here is where you can specify a WMI command you want to run if an alert is triggered.

Create a Scheduled Data Collection Period

1. In Performance Monitor Expand Data Collector Sets

2. Right Click the User Defined Section and Choose New > Data Collector Set

3. Give your collector set a name and choose the Create Manually Option.

4. Click the Create Data Logs radio button, and check a box next to performance counters and click next.

5. The next window asks you which performance counters would you like to monitor, click the Add button.

6. Choose the Counter(s) you would like to monitor and click the add button, click ok when done.

7. The counters you have chosen are listed in the performance counters pane. You do not need to specify any limits, because the data is merely being logged.

8. Choose a Root Directory for your data collector set and click next.

9. Choose whether you want to run as another user or use the default (the System Account), and then decide whether you want to start the data collector set now, save and close, or open the properties of the data collector set.

10. If you would like to create a schedule immediately, choose the option to open the properties of the data collector set.

11. Navigate to the schedule tab and click the add button.

12. Input the desired schedule

13. If you would like to specify a overall duration or other stop condition for the data collector set, click on the stop conditions tab and select your options.

Generate Reports of System Information:

Although you can create a custom Data Collector Set that gathers specific pieces of system information that you specify, the task requires you know the various registry keys that pull the desired info. I would recommend using the predefined template and then removing items you do not need from within. Follow the following steps to perform this task...

1. In Performance Monitor Expand Data Collector Sets

2. Right Click the User Defined Section and Choose New > Data Collector Set

3. Give your Collector set a name, and choose the Create from template option.

4. Choose the System Diagnostics option and click next.

5. Choose a root directory and click next.

6. Choose whether you want to run as another user or use the default (the System Account), and then decide whether you want to start the data collector set now, save and close, or open the properties of the data collector set.

7. To edit what information is gathered by the Data Collector simply select it in the list and then add / remove counters or configuration objects.

8. Right Click the Data Collector and click start when you are ready to run.

9. Data is collected for 60 seconds and then a report is generated in the reports section of Performance Monitor

10. Right-Click the Data Collector Set and Choose the Latest Report option to view the collectors findings.

Create / Use a Data Collector Set Template:

So you've created a custom data collector set that is just right for your environment, and you would like to publish a template of it on a shared drive for your fellow technicians to use. This is quite easily done as shown below.

1. Right click the desired collector set and choose the save as template option

2. Give the XML file a name and save it to a central location for all to access.

To load a custom data collector set template simply...

1. Expand Data Collector Sets

2. Right Click the User Defined Section and Choose New > Data Collector Set

3. Give your Collector set a name, and choose the Create from template option.

4. Click the Browse Button and find the custom template. The rest of the steps are the same as previously outlined.

Create Event Trace Sessions:

Event Tracing is mainly used by programmers as an aid in debugging problems with applications, or finding bottlenecks in processes or components within an application. It can also be used as a way to log additional information when an error occurs. If you want more detailed information about why a program is having an issue, this is the place to look. To create an event trace session you will need to...

1. In Performance Monitor Expand Data Collector Sets

2. Right Click the User Defined Section and Choose New > Data Collector Set

3. Give your collector set a name and choose the Create Manually Option.

4. Click the Create Data Logs radio button, and check a box next to Event Trace Data and click next.

Chapter 12 - Windows Media Player

Window Media Player in Windows 7 is new and improved. By default it is already pinned right on your Suberbar too as shown in Figure 12.1. It is the highlighted icon with the book and arrow pointing to the right.

Figure 12.1

The use features are generally the same as previous version except for a much glassier look. Since Windows 7 is focused around security, in this section we will learn about using customization to configure privacy options in Windows Media Player. Let's take a quick look at the new Windows Media Player as shown in Figure 12.2.

Figure 12.2

Libraries

Notice in the top right hand corner of the screen in Figure 12.2 there are three boxes with an arrow. That is a button that will take you instantly to your Libraries. A new feature in Windows 7 and has its own icon on the Superbar by default which is the icon with a folder as shown in Figure 12.1. Let's look at this new feature in Figure 12.3.

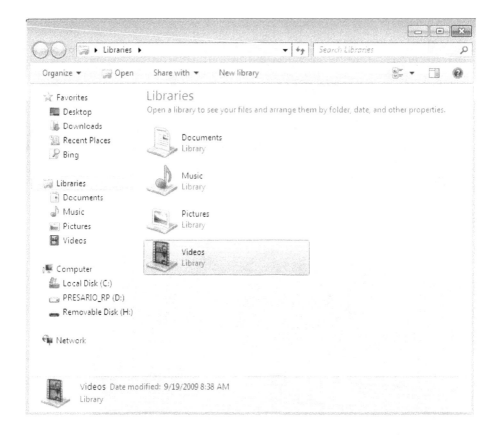

Figure 12.3

This is the new equivalent of Windows Explorer in Windows 7. In Figure 12.4, let's take a more graphical look as this is the only way I think we can identify all the features of the Library.

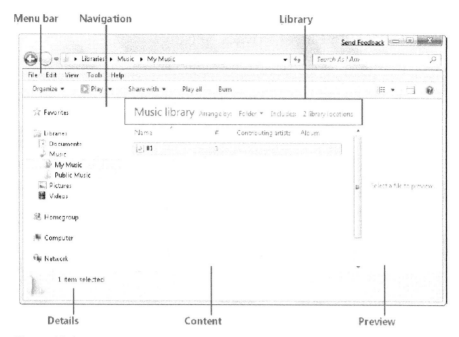

Figure 12.4

Windows Media Player Privacy Settings

Internet Explorer and many other programs gather and send data about what we do to people we don't know and without our knowledge. It almost makes me upset how many programs do this. And not always for marketing purposes either.

Now we can do something about it. To configure privacy settings, when setting up WMP11 for the first time, click on the Windows Media Player icon on the Superbar or go to Start, Programs, and Windows Media Player. Then select Custom Settings and click Next as shown in Figure 12.5.

Figure 12.5

In Figure 12.6 you can adjust the privacy options to your liking. Review the screenshot for my recommendations. The current settings shown are my personal recommendations.

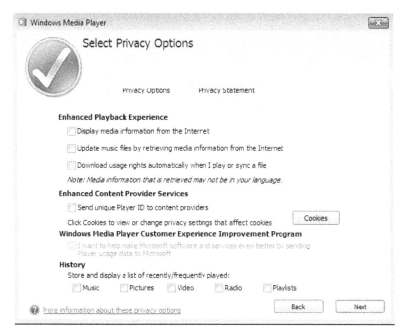

Figure 12.6

Once you are have started Windows Media Player you can adjust the Privacy Settings by right clicking on the display bar and choosing More Options, then the Privacy Tab as shown in Figure 12.7.

Figure 12.7

With these settings your privacy is now protected when viewing and listening to media on the Internet or the local network.

Chapter 13 -Computer Management

The Computer Management console is used primarily for administrators but has some pretty nice features and can help you understand what is going on with your Windows 7 computer. In this section we will look at the following:

- Schedule a task
- Event Viewer
- Local Users and Groups
- Performance Monitor
- Device Manager
- Disk Management

Schedule a task

You must be logged on as an administrator account to perform these steps. If you use a specific program on a regular basis, you can use the Task Scheduler wizard to create a task that opens the program for you automatically. For example we have a server that needs to be rebooted at a certain time of the week, every Friday. That reboot can now be made an automated task as shown in Figure 13.1.

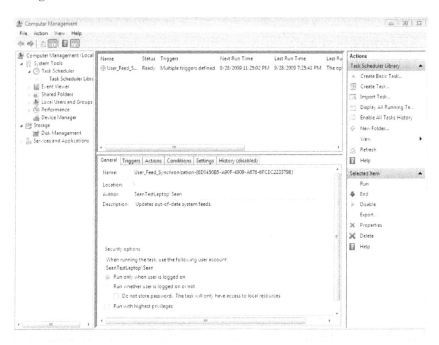

Figure 13.1

To configure a Task, click the Action menu, and then click Create Basic Task. Type the name you want to use for the task. You can also enter an optional description, and then click Next.

> **NOTE:** *To select a schedule to run Daily, Weekly, Monthly, or One time, click Next; specify the schedule you want to use, and then click Next again.*
>
> *To schedule a task based on common recurring events, click, "When the computer starts", or "When you log on", and then click Next. If there are specific events, click "When a specific event is logged", click Next; specify the event log and other information using the drop-down lists, and then click Next.*

To schedule a program to start automatically, simply select Start a program, and then click Next. Then click Browse to find the program you want to start, and then click Next again and then click Finish.

Event Viewer

Event viewer as shown in Figure 13.2 is a viewer that allows you to read log files which are files that record events on your computer system including errors from programs, operating system errors, configuration errors, and user errors. Whenever these types of events occur, Windows records the event in an event log. The event log helps administrator find the detailed explanations of the cause of this issues.

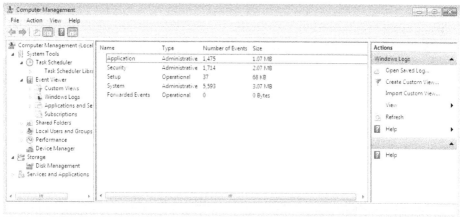

Figure 13.2

Windows Logs include: classifies the system error events in to issues such as an error, warning, or information, depending on the severity of the event.

Event viewer can also be accessed from Control Panel, System and Security, then Administrative Tools. As shown in Figure 13.3.

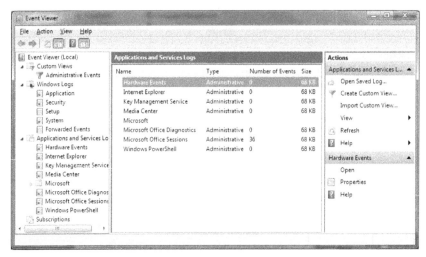

Figure 13.3

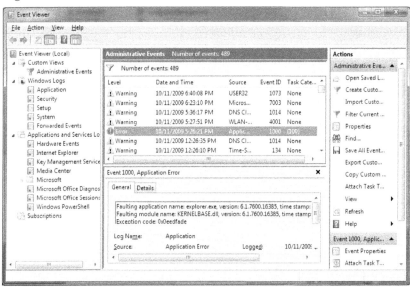

Figure 13.4

Administrative Events

Events are classified as error, warning, or information, depending on the severity of the event. An error is a significant problem, such as loss of data. A warning is an event that isn't necessarily significant, but might indicate a possible future problem. An information event describes the successful operation of a program, driver, or service.

Security-related events

These events are called audits and are described as successful or failed depending on the event, such as whether a user trying to log on to Windows was successful.

Setup events. Computers that are configured as domain controllers will have additional logs displayed here.

System events. System events are logged by Windows and Windows system services, and are classified as error, warning, or information.

Forwarded events. These events are forwarded to this log by other computers.

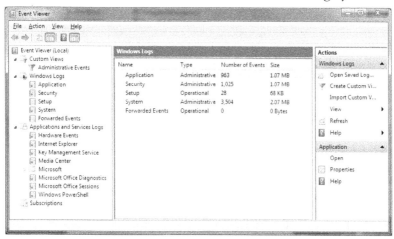

Figure 13.5

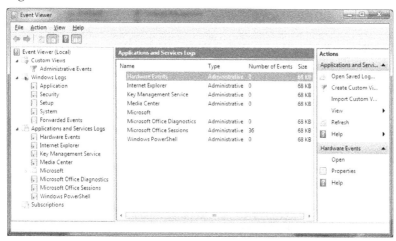

Figure 13.6

Local Users and Groups

Here you can create users that can log in to the computer or user accounts that can run services.

A user group is a collection user accounts can be a member of more than one security, global, or domain group. A user account is often referred to by the user group that it is in such as the administrator account. you can create custom user groups, move accounts from one group to another, and add or remove accounts from different groups. When you create a custom user group, you can choose which rights to assign.

You can create a user named Admin but until you add that user to the Administrators Group on the local PC he is a regular user with hardly any rights as shown in Figure 13.6.

Figure 13.7

Performance Monitor

Performance Monitor is found in Windows 7, Windows Server 2008 R2, and Windows Vista. It is a powerful tool to help you visualize your PC's performance data in real time or from a log file. Performance Monitor allows you to examine the data it collects in a graph, histogram, or report as shown Figure 13.7. You can run Performance Monitor either on the PC or remotely from another PC or server.

> **ALERT:** *Your user account must be included in the local Performance Log Users group to complete this procedure.*

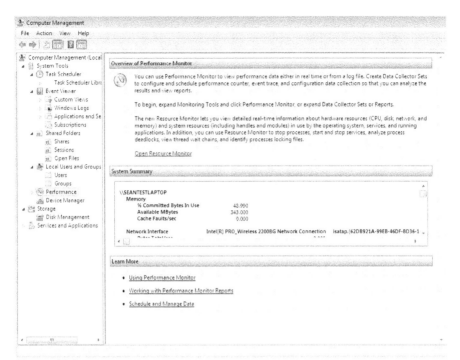

Figure 13.8

Device Manager

Device Manager as shown in Figure B.5 allows you to view and update the device drivers installed on your computer. You can also check to see if hardware is properly installed or modify the current hardware settings.

Figure 13.9

NOTE: *You can open Device Manager: Click the Start button. In the search box, type Device Manager, and then, in the list of results, click Device Manager.*

Disk Management

Disk Manager as shown in Figure 13.10 is a utility that manages the system disks, volumes and partitions on the PC. With Disk Management, you can initialize disks; create volumes, format volumes with file systems FAT, exFAT, FAT32 or NTFS. You can also extend a disk, reduce a disk, check if a disk is healthy or unhealthy, create partitions, delete partitions, or change a drive letter.

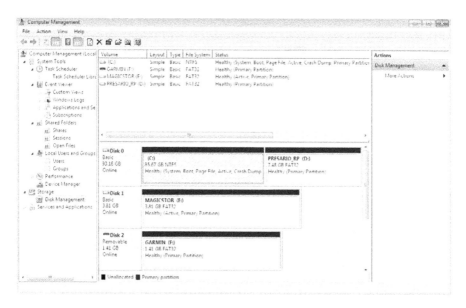

Figure 13.10

Alert: *Windows help does not have detailed information on how to use this feature. This topic is covered in detail in the Windows 7 Professional – The Little Black Book or you can see:*

http://windows7forums.com/windows-7-software/2076-disk-manager.html

Shrink Volume

1. Open the Control Panel (All Items view), and click on the Administrative Tools icon. (Close the Control Panel window.)

2. Click on Computer Management in Administrative Tools, then close the Administrative Tools window.

3. In the left pane under Storage, click on Disk Management.

4. In the middle pane, right click on the partition that you want to shrink and click on Shrink Volume as shown below in Figure 13.11.

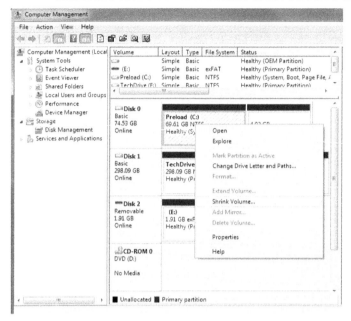

Figure 13.11

1. The utility will run and display how much space the utility can create as shown below in Figure 13.12.

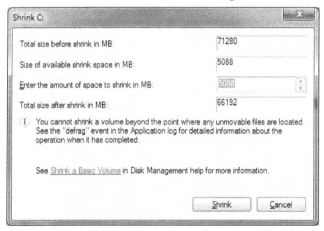

Figure 13.12

6. After you click Shrink, the selected partition will be shrunk and a new empty unallocated space will be created.

Creating A Partition or Volume

1. In Computer Management click Storage, click on Disk Management.

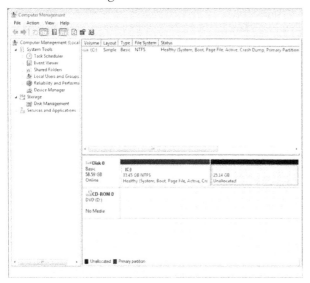

Figure 13.13

2. In the middle pane as shown in Figure 13.13, right click on the empty unallocated partition or volume and click on New Simple Volume.

3. Click on the Next button.

4. Next create a Simple Volume. Identify how many MB (1 GB = 1024 MB) you want to use from the unallocated partition to create the new partition, and then click on the Next button.

5. Select an available drive letter that you want the drive to be assigned to.

6. Choose whether to format the drive with FAT or NTFS, enter the volume label name, and check the "Perform a quick format" box, and click on the Next button as shown in Figure 13.14.

Figure 13.14 (Below)

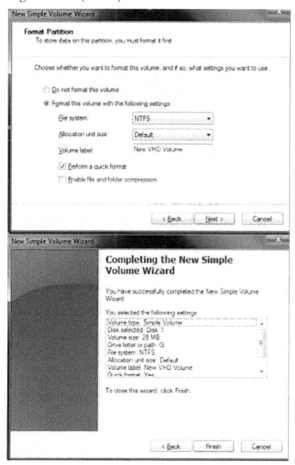

Figure 13.15 (Above)

7. As shown in Figure 13.15, all the information you entered is summed up and will create the simple volume when you press Finish.

Extend Volume

If you have too small a partition and have available unallocated space, you can increase the size of a partition. Right-click the partition, select "Extend Volume," and enter the amount of extra space required. Windows 7 may impose limits on the amount of space that can be added.

Delete Volume

If you are certain that you no longer need the contents of a partition or volume, and would like to use it differently, right-click on the partition and select "Delete Volume." Accept the warning by clicking "OK" to delete the partition.

Change Drive Letter

Change a drive letter. Right-click on a partition and select "Change drive letters and paths." The current drive letter will display. The "Add" button typically allows the partition to be placed inside an existing NTFS folder. Click "Change" to assign a new drive letter. Windows 7 will disallow any changes if the partition is currently used as a system, boot, or pagefile drive.

Administrative Tools

In Figure 13.16 you see a list of the tools in Administrative Tools. You can easily find it by going to the Start Bar and typing Admiistrative Tools in the search area.

Figure 13.15

Let's look at a description of each tool:

Component Services

Configure and administer Component Object Model (COM) components. Component Services is designed for use by developers and administrators.

Computer Management

Allows you to manage local or remote computers using a single, consolidated desktop tool. Using Computer Management, you can perform many tasks, such as monitoring system events, configuring hard disks, managing system performance, and more.

Data Sources (ODBC)

Use Open Database Connectivity (ODBC) to move data from one type of database (a data source) to another.

Event Viewer

View information about significant events, such as a program starting or stopping, or a security error, which are recorded in event logs.

iSCSI Initiator

Allows you to configure advanced connections between storage devices on a network.

Local Security Policy

Allows you to view and edit Group Policy security settings.

Performance Monitor

Allows you to view advanced system information about the central processing unit (CPU), memory, hard disk, and network performance.

Print Management

Allows you to manage printers and print servers on a network and perform other administrative tasks.

Services

Allows you to manage the different services that run in the background on your computer.

System Configuration

Allows you to identify problems that might be preventing Windows from running correctly. For more information, see Using System Configuration.

Task Scheduler

Allows you to schedule programs or other tasks to run automatically. For more information, see Schedule a task.

Windows Firewall with Advanced Security

Allows you to configure advanced firewall settings on both this computer and on remote computers in your network.

Windows Memory Diagnostic

Allows you to check your computer's memory to see if it's functioning properly.

Formatting Your Volume

FAT16

The FAT16 file system was introduced way back with MS–DOS in 1981, and it's showing its age. It was designed originally to handle files on a floppy drive, and has had minor modifications over the years so it can handle hard disks, and even file names longer than the original limitation of 8.3 characters, but it's still the lowest common denominator. The biggest advantage of FAT16 is that it is compatible across a wide variety of operating systems, including Windows 95/98/Me, OS/2, Linux, and some versions of UNIX. The biggest problem of FAT16 is that it has a fixed maximum number of clusters per partition, so as hard disks get bigger and bigger, the size of each cluster has to get larger. In a 2–GB partition, each cluster is 32 kilobytes, meaning that even the smallest file on the partition will take up 32 KB of space. FAT16 also doesn't support compression, encryption, or advanced security using access control lists.

FAT32

The FAT32 file system, was originally introduced in Windows 95 Service Pack 2, is really just an extension of the original FAT16 file system that provides for a much larger number of clusters per partition. As such, it greatly improves the overall disk utilization when compared to a FAT16 file system.

NTFS

The NTFS file system, introduced in Windows NT, is a completely different file system from FAT. It provides for greatly increased security, file–by–file compression, quotas, and even encryption. It is the default file system for new installations of Windows 7, and if you're doing an upgrade from a previous version of Windows, you'll be asked if you want to convert your existing file systems to NTFS.

The NTFS file system is generally not compatible with other operating systems installed on the *same computer*, nor is it available when you've booted a computer from a floppy disk.

Sidebar: Drawbacks of FAT

If you're running more than one operating system on a single computer you will definitely need to format some of your volumes as FAT. Any programs or data that need to be accessed by more than one operating system on that computer should be stored on a FAT16 or possibly FAT32 volume.

Keep in mind that you have no security for data on a FAT16 or FAT32 volume—anyone with access to the computer can read, change, or even delete any file that is stored on a FAT16 or FAT32 partition. In many cases, this is even possible over a network. So do not store sensitive files on drives or partitions formatted with FAT file systems.

exFAT

Extended file allocation table (exFAT) is a new file system that is better adapted to the growing needs of mobile personal storage. The exFAT file system not only handles large files, such as those used for media storage, it enables seamless interoperability between desktop PCs and devices such as portable media devices so that files can easily be copied between desktop and device.

The exFAT system offers the following advantages:

- Enables the file system to handle growing capacities in media, increasing capacity to 32 GB and larger.

- Handles more than 1000 files in a single directory.

- Speeds up storage allocation processes.

- Removes the previous file size limit of 4 GB.

- Supports interoperability with future desktop OSs.

- Provides an extensible format, including OEM-definable parameters to customize the file system for specific device characteristics.

DirectAccess Overview

DirectAccess is a brand new feature in the Windows 7 and Windows Server® 2008 R2 operating systems that gives users the experience of being seamlessly connected to their corporate network any time they have Internet access.

DirectAccess enabled, requests for corporate resources (such as e-mail servers, shared folders, or intranet Web sites) are securely directed to the corporate network, without requiring users to connect to a virtual private network (VPN). DirectAccess provides increased productivity for a mobile workforce by offering the same connectivity experience both in and outside of the office.

Businesses can also benefit from DirectAccess in many ways with new and improved manageability of remote users. Without DirectAccess, computer professionals at the business could only manage mobile computers when users connect to a VPN or physically enter the office.

With DirectAccess they can now manage the mobile computers by updating Group Policy settings and distributing software updates any time the mobile computer has Internet connectivity, even if the user is not logged on.

Taking advantage of technologies such as Internet Protocol version 6 (IPv6) and Internet Protocol security (IPsec), DirectAccess provides secure and flexible network infrastructure for enterprises. Let's look at a list of DirectAccess security and performance capabilities:

- Better authentication: DirectAccess authenticates the computer, enabling the computer to connect to the intranet before the user logs on and can also authenticate the user and supports two-factor authentication using smart cards.

- Encryption: DirectAccess uses IPsec to provide encryption for communications across the Internet.

- Better access control: Computer support professionals can configure the intranet resources differently for users. Allowing individual users or a group of users access use specific applications, servers or even subnets.

- Simplification and Cost Reduction. DirectAccess separates intranet from Internet traffic, which reduces unnecessary traffic on the corporate network by sending only traffic destined for the corporate network through the DirectAccess server.

File Permissions

For the exam there are a couple of things you need to know regarding file permissions as we outline here in this section. You need to know how to change file permissions or object permissions and how to take ownership of a file or object when you don't have permissions to access them but you are an administrator.

How to Take Ownership in Windows 7

There may be a time when you need to take ownership of a file away from another Windows 7 user. To gain access, move, or copy a file or folder. To do this, follow these instructions.

1. Locate the file or folder on which you want to take ownership in Windows Explorer.

2. Right click on the file or the folder and select "Properties" from Context Menu as shown in Figure 13.16

3. Click on Security tab

Figure 13.16

4. Click on "Advanced"

5. Now click on **"Owner"** tab in Advance Security Settings for the User you want to take ownership with. This must be an administrator account as shown in Figure 13.17.

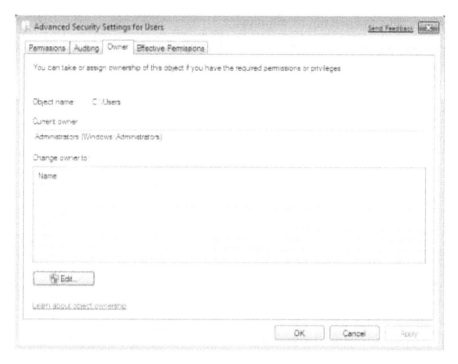

Figure 13.17

6. Click on the "Edit" Button and select a user or group and enter the name of a user or group and click "ok" as shown in Figure 13.18. This provides a space for you to type the object names that you want to find. You can search for multiple objects by separating each name with a semicolon. Use one of the following syntax examples:

- DisplayName (example: FirstName LastName)
- ObjectName (example: Computer1)
- UserName (example: User)
- ObjectName@DomainName (example: User@Domain)
- DomainName\ObjectName (example: Domain\User)

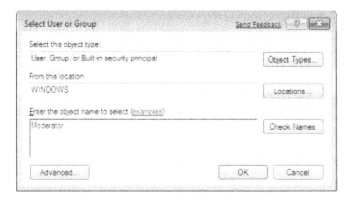

Figure 13.18

8. Select a User or group from the options given from the system to the names of users or groups that match the name or names you entered. Click "apply" and the "ok."

> **NOTE:** You will need to check "Replace owner on subcontainers and objects" if you have files and folder within selected folder".)

9. Click "ok" when Windows Security Prompt is displayed as shown in Figure 13.19.

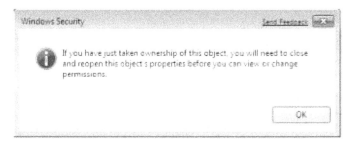

Figure 13.19

10. Verify the owner name has changed.

11. Click **"Ok"** to exit from Properties.

Once you have taken the ownership of file or folder you Grant Permissions to that file/folder or object. Let's take a look at how to do this in the next section.

How to Grant Permissions in Windows 7

Now let's take a look at how to add/grant permissions to a file or object in Windows 7:

1. Locate the file, folder, or object which you want to change the permissions on in a file windows, search window or in Windows Explorer

2. Right click on file or folder and select "Properties" from Context Menu

3. Click on "Edit" button in Properties windows Click "ok" to confirm UAC elevation request.

4. Select the user or group from the permission window or click "add" to add other users or groups. This provides a space for you to type the object names that you want to find. You can search for multiple objects by separating each name with a semicolon. Use one of the following syntax examples:

- DisplayName (example: FirstName LastName)

- ObjectName (example: Computer1)

- UserName (example: User)

- ObjectName@DomainName (example: User@Domain)

- DomainName\ObjectName (example: Domain\User)

5. Under Permission section shown in Figure 13.20, check the options next to the rights which you want to grant each user or group such as:

Modify
This allows a user or group to change existing files and folders, but cannot create new ones.

Read and execute
This allows a user or group to see the contents of existing files and folders and can run programs in a folder.

Read
This allows a user or group to see the contents of a folder and open files and folders.

Write
This allows a user or group to create new files and folders and make changes to existing files and folders.

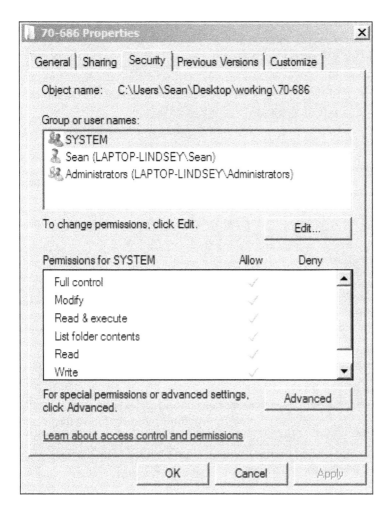

Figure 13.20

> **6.** Click "Ok" for changes to take effect and click "ok " to exit from the Properties window.

The users or groups you assigned permissions to in the previous steps should now be able to access the files, folders or objects you gave permissions to.

Chapter 14-IPv4 and IPv6

We will only go into a brief overview of IP4 and IP6 in this book. For more detailed information on both protocols visit these links:

IPv4

http://en.wikipedia.org/wiki/IPv4#Address_representations

IPv6

http://www.microsoft.com/downloads/details.aspx?FamilyID=CBC0 B8A3-B6A4-4952-BBE6-D976624C257C&displaylang=en

IP Version 4

Although IP stands for Internet Protocol, it's a communications protocol used from the smallest private network to the massive global Internet. An IP address is a unique identifier given to a single device on an IP network. The IP address consists of a 32-bit number that ranges from 0 to 4294967295. This means that theoretically, the Internet can contain approximately 4.3 billion unique objects when using IPv4.

But to make such a large address block easier to handle, it was chopped up into four 8-bit numbers, or "octets," separated by a period. Instead of 32 binary base-2 digits, which would be too long to read, it's converted to four base-256 digits. Octets are made up of numbers ranging from 0 to 255. The numbers below show how IP addresses increment.

0.0.0.0
0.0.0.1
...increment 252 hosts...
0.0.0.254
0.0.0.255
0.0.1.0
0.0.1.1
...increment 252 hosts...
0.0.1.254
0.0.1.255
0.0.2.0
0.0.2.1
...increment 4+ billion hosts...
255.255.255.255

The word subnet is short for sub network--a smaller network within a larger one. The smallest subnet that has no more subdivisions within it is considered a single "broadcast domain," which directly correlates to a single LAN (local area network) segment on an Ethernet switch.

Broadcast Domains

The broadcast domain serves an important function because this is where devices on a network communicate directly with each other's MAC addresses, which don't route across multiple subnets, let alone the entire Internet. MAC address communications are limited to a smaller network because they rely on ARP broadcasting to find their way around, and broadcasting can be scaled only so much before the amount of broadcast traffic brings down the entire network with sheer broadcast noise. For this reason, the most common smallest subnet is 8 bits, or precisely a single octet, although it can be smaller or slightly larger.

Subnets

Subnets have a beginning and an ending, and the beginning number is always even and the ending number is always odd. The beginning number is the "Network ID" and the ending number is the "Broadcast ID."

You're not allowed to use these numbers because they both have special meaning with special purposes. The Network ID is the official designation for a particular subnet, and the ending number is the broadcast address that every device on a subnet listens to. Anytime you want to refer to a subnet, you point to its Network ID and its subnet mask, which defines its size. Anytime you want to send data to everyone on the subnet (such as a multicast), you send it to the Broadcast ID.

Subnets can be subdivided into smaller subnets and even smaller ones still. The most important thing to know about chopping up a network is that you can't arbitrarily pick the beginning and ending. The chopping must be along clean binary divisions. Let's take a look at the subnets in Figure 14.1

Subnet mask quick reference							
Host Bit length	math	Max hosts	Subnet mask	Mask octet	Binary mask	Mask length	Subnet length
0	$2^0=$	1	255.255.255.255	4	11111111	32	0
1	$2^1=$	2	255.255.255.254	4	11111110	31	1
2	$2^2=$	4	255.255.255.252	4	11111100	30	2
3	$2^3=$	8	255.255.255.248	4	11111000	29	3
4	$2^4=$	16	255.255.255.240	4	11110000	28	4
5	$2^5=$	32	255.255.255.224	4	11100000	27	5
6	$2^6=$	64	255.255.255.192	4	11000000	26	6
7	$2^7=$	128	255.255.255.128	4	10000000	25	7
8	$2^8=$	256	255.255.255.0	3	11111111	24	8
9	$2^9=$	512	255.255.254.0	3	11111110	23	9
10	$2^{10}=$	1024	255.255.252.0	3	11111100	22	10
11	$2^{11}=$	2048	255.255.248.0	3	11111000	21	11
12	$2^{12}=$	4096	255.255.240.0	3	11110000	20	12
13	$2^{13}=$	8192	255.255.224.0	3	11100000	19	13
14	$2^{14}=$	16384	255.255.192.0	3	11000000	18	14
15	$2^{15}=$	32768	255.255.128.0	3	10000000	17	15
16	$2^{16}=$	65536	255.255.0.0	2	11111111	16	16
17	$2^{17}=$	131072	255.254.0.0	2	11111110	15	17
18	$2^{18}=$	262144	255.252.0.0	2	11111100	14	18
19	$2^{19}=$	524288	255.248.0.0	2	11111000	13	19
20	$2^{20}=$	1048576	255.240.0.0	2	11110000	12	20
21	$2^{21}=$	2097152	255.224.0.0	2	11100000	11	21
22	$2^{22}=$	4194304	255.192.0.0	2	11000000	10	22
23	$2^{23}=$	8388608	255.128.0.0	2	10000000	9	23
24	$2^{24}=$	16777216	255.0.0.0	1	11111111	8	24

Figure 14.1

Subnet Mask Role

The subnet mask plays a crucial role in defining the size of a subnet. Take a look at Figure 14.1. Notice the pattern and pay special attention to the numbers in red. Whenever you're dealing with subnets, it will come in handy to remember eight special numbers that reoccur when dealing with subnet masks. They are 255, 254, 252, 248, 240, 224, 192, and 128. You'll see these numbers over and over again in IP networking, and memorizing them will make your life much easier.

Determine Default Subnet Mask: Each of Classes A, B and C has a default subnet mask, which is the subnet mask for the network prior to subnetting. It has a 1 for each network ID bit and a 0 for each host ID bit. For Class C, the subnet mask is 255.255.255.0. In binary, this is:

11111111 11111111 11111111 00000000

Change Left-Most Zeroes To Ones For Subnet Bits: We have decided to use 3 bits for the subnet ID. The subnet mask has to have a 1 for each of the network ID or subnet ID bits. The network ID bits are already 1 from the default subnet mask, so, we change the 3 left-most 0 bits in the default subnet mask from a 0 to 1, shown highlighted below. This results in the following custom subnet mask for our network:

11111111 11111111 11111111 11100000

Convert Subnet Mask To Dotted Decimal Notation: We take each of the octets in the subnet mask and convert it to decimal. The result is our custom subnet mask in the form we usually see it: 255.255.255.224.

> **NOTE:** *Express Subnet Mask In "Slash Notation": Alternately, we can express the subnet mask in "slash notation". This is just a slash followed by the number of ones in the subnet mask. 255.255.255.224 is equivalent to "/27".*

The subnet mask not only determines the size of a subnet, but it can also help you pinpoint where the end points on the subnet are if you're given any IP address within that subnet. The reason it's called a subnet "mask" is that it literally masks out the host bits and leaves only the Network ID that begins the subnet. Once you know the beginning of the subnet and how big it is, you can determine the end of the subnet, which is the Broadcast ID.

To calculate the Network ID, you simply take any IP address within that subnet and run the AND operator on the subnet mask. Let's take an IP address of 10.20.237.15 and a subnet mask of 255.255.248.0.

Using Binary Math

The binary version shows how the 0s act as a mask on the IP address on top. Inside the masking box, the 0s convert all numbers on top into zeros, no matter what the number is. When you take the resultant binary Network ID and convert it to decimal, you get 10.20.232.0 as the Network ID.

Often I see computer support technicians in the field using this slow and cumbersome technique to convert everything to binary and then convert back to decimal using the Windows Calculator. But there's a really simple shortcut using the Windows Calculator, since the operator works directly on decimal numbers. Simply punch in 237, hit the AND operator, and then 248 and [Enter] to instantly get 232.. I'll never understand why this isn't explained to students in manuals, because it makes subnet mask calculations a lot easier.

IP Version 6

A brand new Next Generation TCP/IP stack with enhanced support for Internet Protocol version 6 (IPv6) is included in Windows 7. We will take a look at IPv6 and where to configure the IP address settings. This exam does not cover anything beyond that. So this will be a basic overview.

The need for upgrading from IPv4 to IPv6 is driven by a number of reasons. The exponential growth of the Internet is rapidly exhausting the existing IPv4 public address space. A temporary solution to this problem has been found in Network Address Translation (NAT), which is a technology that maps multiple private (intranet) addresses to a single public (Internet) address.

IPv6 uses a 128-bit address, meaning that we have a maximum of 2^{128} addresses available, or:

340,282,366,920,938,463,463,374,607,431,768,211,456

 Probably enough to give multiple IP addresses to every person and grain of sand on the planet. We probably will have enough if we invite several other largely inhabited planets outside our solar system to join us on the World Wide Web.

The IPv6 address space was designed to be hierarchical rather than flat in structure, and routing tables for IPv6 routers will be much smaller and more efficient than those on IPv4 routers.

IPv6 also has enhanced support for Quality of Service (QoS) by including a Traffic Class field in the header to specify how traffic should be handled along with a new Flow Label field in the header that enables routers to identify packets that belong to a particular traffic flow and handle them appropriately.

Anycast

An anycast address is a single address assigned to multiple nodes(computers). A packet sent to an anycast address is then delivered to the first available node. This is a slick way to provide both load-balancing and automated failover.

Basically, an IPv6 packets with anycast destination addresses are delivered to the nearest interface specified by the address. Currently, anycast addresses are assigned only to routers and can only represent destination addresses.

IPv6 Addressing - Address Dissection

An IPv6 address looks like this

2001:0db8:3c4d:0015:0000:0000:abcd:ef12

2001:0db8:3c4d | 0015 | abcd:ef12

Global Prefix | Subnet | Interface ID

Prefix

The prefix identifies it as a global unicast address which has three parts:

- A network identifier
- A subnet
- A interface identifier

The global routing prefix must be assigned to you, either by direct assignment from a Regional Internet Registry like APNIC, ARIN, or RIPE NCC. The subnet and interface IDs are controlled by you, the hardworking local network administrator.

You'll probably be running mixed IPv6/IPv4 networks for some time. IPv6 addresses must total 128 bits. IPv4 addresses are represented like this:

0000:0000:0000:0000:0000:0000:192.168.1.10

Eight blocks of 16 bits each are required in an IPv6 address. The IPv4 address occupies 32 bits, so that is why there are only seven colon-delimited blocks. The localhost address is 0000:0000:0000:0000:0000:0000:0000:0001. Naturally we want shortcuts, because these are long and all those zeroes are just dumb-looking. Leading zeroes can be omitted, and contiguous blocks of zeroes can be omitted entirely as shown below:

2001:0db8:3c4d:0015:0:0:abcd:ef12
2001:0db8:3c4d:0015::abcd:ef12

Lucky for you this exam doesn't cover routing. Just assigning an IP address to an interface. So let's take a look at that in the next section.

Configuring a IPv6 Address

1. Go to the Start Bar, Control Panel, Network and Internet, then choose

Network Sharing.

> **Note**: *You can also Right-click your network connection, and then click Properties. If you are prompted for an administrator password or confirmation, type the password or provide confirmation.*

2. Under Your Active Networks double click on the connection you want to configure as shown in Figure 14.2.

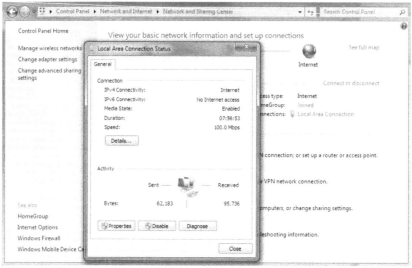

Figure 14.2

3. Click the Properties button and answer '"yes" to any UAC prompts that you get.

4. Select Internet Protocol Version 6 (TCP/IPv6) and click Properties to open the Internet Protocol Version 6 (TCP/IPv6) Properties sheet as shown in Figure 14.3

Figure 14.3

5. Configure the IPv6 settings for the network connection as shown in Figure 14.4. You can also validate the new TCP/IP settings using the Windows Network Diagnostics Troubleshooter. The settings shown allow the computer to get an address from DHCP. I think that it will be only servers that get static IP's as IPv6 has some pretty long numbers.

For more information see:

http://technet.microsoft.com/en-us/library/bb878005.aspx

Chapter 15 - Windows 7 Troubleshooting Centric

Windows 7, unlike previous versions of Windows has an entire section of the Control Panel dedicated to troubleshooting. To Access this section perform the following actions...

1. Click on the Windows ORB (AKA Start Button)

2. In the Right-Pane Click on Control Panel

3. In the System and Security Section of the Control Panel click on Find and Fix Problems

The troubleshooting applet lets you troubleshoot the most common computer problems you will encounter all in one convenient location (Figure 15.5).

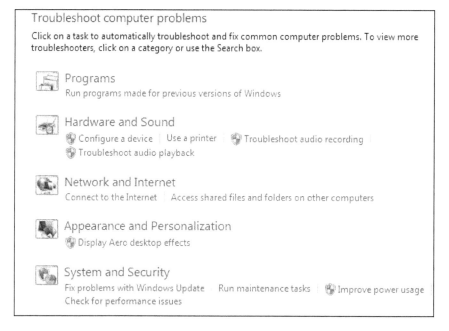

Figure 15.5

At the bottom of the screen of the main troubleshooting applet you will notice a checkbox to **Get the most up-to-date troubleshooters from Windows Online Troubleshooting service** this box should remain checked if you want windows to periodically check for updates for troubleshooters while you are connected to the internet.

Each icon in the troubleshooting applet opens up a program that will attempt to detect and repair problems associated with the description for the program listed in the troubleshooting applet. All of the programs contain an advanced button that lets you choose if you want Windows to automatically repair any problems it encounters.

Windows will then run through a series of tests to determine possible causes of the problem you are experiencing. Once the automated troubleshooting has completed Windows will list any problems it detected as well as its success or failure in fixing the detected problems. You can then choose to view detailed information about what tests Windows performed and the results of the tests in a troubleshooting report as shown in Figure 5.6.

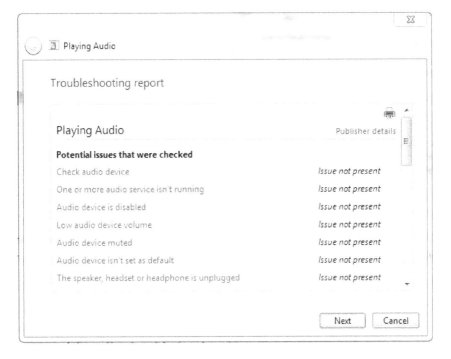

Figure 15.6

The other options you can choose are Close the troubleshooter or Explore additional options.

Explore Additional options brings you to a page offering icons for you to search for a solution in Microsoft's help and support on the local computer, check the Windows communities, Find related troubleshooters, Get Help from a Friend (Remote Assistance), Recovery (System Recovery), or Online Support as show in Figure 15.7.

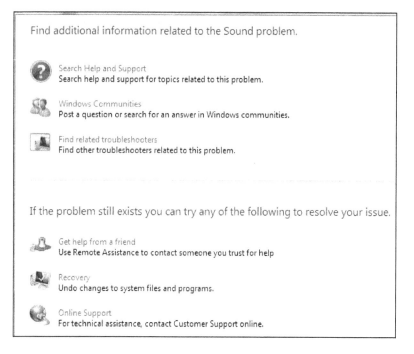

Figure 15.7

Assess Yourself – Are You Ready For the Exam?

Question 1

You are the administrator of a network where all the desktops run Windows XP and are members of an Active Directory Domain Services domain. You have been tasked to migrate all the XP desktops to Windows 7 Professional. Your second task is to deploy a VPN server to support remote network access for the computers. These desktops will need to use remote access during the migration to Windows 7. What should you do?

     A. Set the VPN use port 443.

     B. Set the VPN server to CHAPv2.

     C. Configure the VPN server for 3DES encryption.

     D. Set the VPN server to Layer 2 Tunneling Protocol.

Answer: _____

Question 2

You are the administrator of a network where all the desktops run Windows 7.

The shipping department uses a Wireless Wide Area Network (WWAN), WLAN, and wired network connections to work on laptops at remote location.

The Shipping department has to reestablish their secure connections and restart multiple applications frequently. To ensure unnecessary interruption and make sure that the shipping employees are able to work what should you do?

     A. Configure each portable computer to use the VPN Reconnect feature.

     B. Create a Group Policy to configure preferred wireless access points.

     C. Configure Group Policy preferences to create multiple VPN connections.

     D. Configure each portable computer to use the Extensible Authentication Protocol.

Answer: _____

Question 3

You are the administrator of a network where all the desktops run Windows 7 and are members of an Active Directory Domain Services domain. Using the Task Manager, you discover that the memory usage on the computers is very high. You need to find the reason for the high memory usage. What should you do to determine the cause?

A. Run the Resource Monitor Tool and pay close attention to the content on the Memory tab.

B. Run the Windows Memory Management Diagnostic tool and set the memory scanning feature to graph mode.

C. In the Program Files, choose System Tools, Accessories, and then choose Memory Management Diagnostics and Configuration Tool. Run the default scan of the memory and see what is using the resources.

D. Set a user defined data set and set Memory\Available Mbytes and Memory\% Committed Bytes In Use counters.

Answer: _____

Question 4

You are the administrator of a network where all the desktops run Windows 7 and are members of an Active Directory Domain Services domain.

Several users have requested need hardware upgrades on their PC's. One of the problems noted is that their PC's randomly perform restarts automatically. After you examine one of the computers and verify the following:

- No viruses or malware.

- Only approved applications and processes are installed.

- All windows and software updates to the operating system and applications have been applied to the computer.

You need to immediately find out why the PC's are restarting automatically. What should you do?

A. Run the Boot manager log tool.

B. Run the fixmbr command from the Recovery Console.

C. Run the Windows Memory Diagnostic tool.

D. Remove the autoexec,bat to see if the problem goes away.

Answer: _____

Question 5

You are the administrator of a network where all the desktops run Windows 7 and are members of an Active Directory Domain Services domain. Your company has a policy requiring all unnecessary or unapproved services be disabled on all the computers.

The shipping department has been provided with new wireless mobile broadband adapters.

You need to make sure that computers can connect to the new broadband network. Which service should be enabled on the portable computers?

      A. WLAN AutoConfig

      B. WiFi LAN Tools

      C. The Master Browser service

      D. WWAN AutoConfig

Answer: _____

Question 6

You are the administrator of a network where all the desktops run Windows 7 and are members of an Active Directory Domain Services domain. The preview function which displays the Content view in Windows Explorer and the Search box needs to be disabled on all PC's in the company. What should you do?

      A. Go to Windows Explorer and uncheck the show snippets feature button under File Options.

      B. Set Group Policy to enable the No search results viewer.

      C. Set Group Policy to enable the Turn off the display of snippets in Content view mode setting.

      D. Set Group Policy to enable the Turn off viewer panes.

Answer: _____

Question 7

Your company has a main office and two smaller retail locations located out of state. All of the computers in your company's network all run Windows 7, connect to a Windows Server 2008 domain and are members of an Active Directory Domain Services domain. All the servers in the network environment use Windows Server 2008 R2 and are located in the main office location. Your retail office employees use a small 256K partial T1 link which is slow because of the amount of traffic and there is high latency accessing files on the network share located at the main office. You are tasked to do the following:

3. Reduce WAN link usage.

4. Lessen the latency user have when trying to accessing files at the main office.

What should you do?

A. Configure BranchCache in Distributed Mode on a Windows Server 2008 R2 server.

B. The BranchCache service should be configured to start automatically on a Windows 2008 Server.

C. Change the MTU size on the server running ISA or Routing and Remote Access.

D. Configure Quality of Service (QoS) on the Windows 2008 Server running Routing and Remote Access for the domain

Answer: _____

Question 8

All client computers on your company network run Windows 7 and are members of an Active Directory Domain Services domain. All servers in the network are running Windows Server 2008 R2 and are located in the headquarters. A remote office connects to the main office by using a cellular network.

Employees at the remote office frequently download a daily report from an IIS Web server at the main office, which causes them to incur excessive pay per bandwidth usage costs. You need to decrease the network bandwidth usage costs incurred by the remote office. What should you do?

A. Implement Direct Access.

B. Implement Readyboost.

C. Implement Distributed File System.

D. Configure Branch Cache mode.

Answer: _____

Question 9

All client computers on your company network run Windows 7 and are members of an Active Directory Domain Services domain. All the laptop users in the network connect only to the 802.1X-authenticated wireless network. Wireless settings are set through the MediaWorksPublishing.com's Group Policy.

You discover that new laptops are not able to join to the domain. What should you do to allow the computers to join the domain?

> A. Connect the portable computers to the domain by Branche Cache security authentication.

> B. Connect the portable computers to the wireless network by using a hidden profile.

> C. Connect the portable computers to the domain by using bio identification characteristics.

> D. Connect the portable computers to the wireless network by using a Bootstrap Profile.

Answer: _____

Question 10

All client computers on your company network run Windows 7 and are members of an Active Directory Domain Services domain. All servers in the network are running Windows Server 2008 R2. Employees use a VPN connection to connect to the company's headquarters from a remote location.

Employees remain connected to the VPN server to browse the Internet, even for personal use. This is becoming an issue and you are instructed to make sure that remote users cannot use the Internet while connected to the VPN. What should you do?

> A. Configure the VPN connection eliminating all DNS entries.

> B. Configure the DHCP to stop assigning IP addresses when connecting through the VPN.

> C. Use Group Policy to disable the Use default gateway on remote network setting on each client computer.

> D. Use Group Policy to block port 80 on the firewall on each computer connecting through the VPN.

Answer: _____

Question 11

All of the computers in your company's network all run Windows 7 and connect to a Windows Server 2008 domain. You plan to use Group Policy to enable BitLocker Drive Encryption (BDE) with the following requirements:

3. The BitLocker recovery keys are stored in a single centralized location. ·

4. All data is encrypted but only after a backup of the recovery key is available.

Which of the following should be done?

A. BitLocker /keystore command from a Command Prompt.

B. Using the BitLocker Wizard choose the Default Folder option for secure password storage and identify the location the shared keys should be stored.

C. From the Action menu option choose Enable BitLocker encrypted drive recovery key. Then replace the default local drive selection with a secure network share.

D. Use the Active Directory Domain Services setting to enable the Store BitLocker recovery information.

Answer: _____

Question 12

There is an Active Directory domain and a Direct Access infrastructure already configured in your network. Windows 7 is installed on a new laptop and you have joined the computer to the domain. You have to make sure that the computer can establish DirectAccess connections. Which of the following should be performed?

A. Create Network Discovery firewall exception should be enabled.

B. Add the users to the Remote Operators group.

C. Create a VPN connection new network connection should be created.

D. Install a valid computer certificate.

Answer: _____

Question 13

All client computers on your company network run Windows 7 and are members of an Active Directory Domain Services domain. Employees use Windows Internet Explorer 8 to access the Internet. Users believe that their computers are infected with malicious software which you soon confirm. As the network administrator you are tasked to configure the settings in Internet Explorer 8 to prevent malicious software from being installed on the computers. What should you do?

      A. Configure Popup Blocker.

      B. Configure SmartScreen Filter.

      C. Restrict access to the Local intranet zone.

      D. Implement a content filter on the firewall.

Answer: _____

Question 14

You use a laptop named Laptop1 which runs Windows 7. There is a Windows 2008 R2 server named Server1 that contains a shared folder named Data. You need to configure Laptop1 to cache and encrypt the files from the Data share so they can be used when Laptop1 is not connected to the network. You want the files in the Data share to automatically synch each time Laptop1 connects to the network. Which action should be performed?

      A. On Server1, the files should be encrypted on the Data share. Copy the data to a folder on the Laptop1.

      B. Copy the files from the Data share to the Documents library and turn on BitLocker To Go Drive Encryption.

      C. You should make the Data share available offline and enable encryption of offline files on Laptop1.

      D. BitLocker Drive Encryption should be configured on Server1. You should make Data share available offline on all computers in the network.

Answer: _____

Question 15

All client computers on your company network run Windows 7 and are members of an Active Directory Domain Services domain. Employees using laptops report that they get connected to a public wireless network from the company conference room.

You need to ensure that the employees connect to the company wireless network by default from anywhere within the company premises.

What should you do?

> A. Configure the Network authentication setting to allow MAC authentication.
>
> B. Rename your wireless SSID with starting with an "A" so it falls before the public wireless networks SSID.
>
> C. Apply a Wireless Network Policy to set the company wireless network as the preferred network.
>
> D. Apply a Group Policy to allow only the network SSID.

Answer: _____

Question 16

You have two computers named Laptop1 and Computer2. Windows Vista is run on Laptop1. Windows 7 is run on Computer2. You are tasked with migrating all the users files and profiles from Laptop1 to Computer2. Which command would be used to identify how much space is required to complete the migration?

A. Run Windows Easy Migrate and press test the C: drive on Laptop1.

B. dsmigrate \\Laptop1\store /nocompress /p should be run on Computer2.

C. loadstate \\Laptop1\store /nocompress should be run on Computer2.

D. scanstate c:\store /nocompress /p should be run on Laptop1.

Answer: _____

Question 17

All client computers on your company network run Windows 7 and are members of an Active Directory Domain Services domain. All servers in the network are running Windows Server 2008 R2. You need to ensure that data stored on removable drives is encrypted. What should you do?

A. Set the Removable Disks:Apply only BitLocker encryption.

B. Set the Control use of BitLocker on removable drives option to Allow users to apply BitLocker on removable drives by using Group Policy.

C. Set Group Policy to enable Configure use of passwords for removable data drives

D. None Of The Above

Answer: _____

Question 18

You have a workgroup which contains seven computers running Windows 7 Professional. A computer named Computer1 has MP4 files to share. What should Computer 1, do to share the files? (Choose 2.)

A. Connect a removable drive and enable BitLocker To Go.

B. Create a Homegroup with a shared password.

C. All BranchCache rules should be enabled in Windows Firewall.

D. The files should be moved to a Media Library.

Answer: _____

Question 19

The Aero Shake feature will work if which of the following conditions are met? (Choose 2.)

A. A display adapter compatible with WDDM is installed.

B. Aero features are downloaded from Microsoft.

C. The windows experience index is at least 2.

D. The Windows Experience Index is 3 or greater.

Answer: _____

Question 20

All client computers on your company network run Windows 7 and are members of an Active Directory Domain Services domain. All computers are configured to automatically download and install Windows updates. You are the network administrator of a network which requires a proxy server for access to the Internet but does not use the Web Proxy Auto-Discovery (WPAD).

Another network technician notices that none of the networks computers are receiving installed updates. What should you do to fix the issue and allow the computers to automatically install updates?

A. Set Automatic Updates to install through WSUS.

B. Set Automatic Updates to override proxy settings and use an administrator account.

C. Run the proxycfg.exe tool on each computer on the network segment.

D. Log on to each computer on the network segment as Administrator and configure an Internet Explorer proxy manually.

Answer: _____

Question 21

All client computers on your company network run Windows 7 and are members of an Active Directory Domain Services domain. Employees access websites each day by using Windows Internet Explorer 8. As the network administrator you notice employees are accessing restricted websites, by modifying the security levels assigned to Internet zones. Your supervisor wants you to stop employees from modifying the security levels. What should you do?

A. Disable the Protected Security Group Policy setting for Internet Explorer.

B. Disable the Zone Elevation Protection Group Policy setting.

C. Modify the Group Policy option and enable the Zone Elevation Protection setting.

D. Enable the Group Policy setting called Do Not allow user to enable users from modifying Internet Explorer Policies.

Answer: _____

Question 22

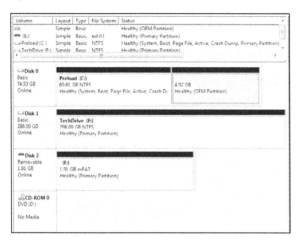

You have a computer that runs Windows 7. You open the Disk Management in the Computer Management MMC. You need to make sure that you are able to create a new partition on Disk 0 but the space is used. Which of the following would allow you to make another partition on Disk 0, as shown in the Figure above?

    A. Create a Virtual Hard Disk (VHD) and assign as Disk 0. Change Disk 0 to Disk 3.

    B. In order to make sure of this, volume C should be compressed.

    C. In order to make sure of this, Disk 0 should be converted into a dynamic disk.

    D. Shrink volume C to make space for another volume.

Answer: _____

Question 23

All client computers on your company network run Windows 7 and are members of an Active Directory Domain Services domain. Employees log on to their computers as Standard users. A malicious software attack is affecting your network users. Many users are receiving User Account Control (UAC) messages frequently requesting permission to elevate privileges. You know that the malicious software attack is responsible for these UAC prompts and need to ensure that employees are unable to provide elevated credentials. Which of the following should you do?

A. Configure the Group Policy User Account Control to enable the UAC only elevate for Administrator logins.

B. Configure the Group Policy User Account Control to enable the "Secure desktop for Standard users prompt."

C. Configure the Group Policy User Account Control: called "Behavior of the elevation prompt for standard users setting to automatically deny elevation requests."

D. Turn off the UAC prompt by modifying each computers security settings in the Control panel.

Answer: _____

Question 24

There is an Active Directory domain in your network. There are two computers which have already joined the domain named Computer1 and Computer 2 running Windows 7 Professional. From Computer 1, you can recover all *Encrypting File System (EFS)* encrypted files for users in the domain. You have to make sure that you can recover all EFS encrypted files from Computer 2. What action should you perform?

A. Use the Cipher.exe /wc:\. The take the certificate and place it on Computer 2 to be able to read the encrypted files.

B. Use AppLocker to create a data recovery certificate on Computer1 and copy the certificate to Computer2.

C. Export the data using the new Windows 7 EFS Recovery tool using the /export syntax on Computer 1 and using the /target syntax for Computer 2.

D. Export the Data Recovery Agent Certificate on Computer 1 to Computer 2.

Answer: _____

Question 25

All client computers on your company network run Windows 7 and are members of an Active Directory Domain Services domain. All servers in the network are running Windows Server 2008 R2.

You are finding that someone has a burned CD that has a virus that is installing automatically. You need to ensure that virus does not automatically run on the computers. What should you do to fix this?

A. Disable the Windows Installer service from the Domain Controller.

B. Use Group policy and enable the "Disable the Autoplay function".

C. Set the auto SHIFT press for CD's configured in a Active Directory domain script.

D. Prevent the installation of unsigned applications by requiring a certificate by enabling the Security Certificate service on the server.

Answer: _____

Question 26

After the installation of third-party software you find the Original Equipment Manufacturer (OEM) recovery partition is no longer installed on the PC. The Boot Configuration Database (BCD) has also been corrupted. You need to repair the BCD so that the computers can boot up. What should you do?

A. Create a new system repair disc and run the Startup Repair recovery tool.

B. Run the System Image Recovery tool from the Windows 7 Professional or the Windows 7 Ultimate DVD.

C. Select the Last Known Good Configuration after booting the PC.

D. You will need to reinstall Windows 7 to replace the BCD.

Answer: _____

Question 27

All client computers on your company network run Windows 7 and are members of an Active Directory Domain Services domain. The shipping department staffs run an application that collects data from 09:30 hours to 15:00 hours every day to transmit shipping information. After the data collection, the application generates reports from the information.

While the PC is generating reports, the shipping department staff experience slow performance on their computers. You discover that the usage of the processor on the computer is between 85 and 100 percent. What should you do to increase the speed of the PC's during the generation of the reports?

    A. Add a USB processor.

    B. Use Virtual Server to offset some of the processing on the CPU.

    C. Add more RAM to buffer the waiting data to the CPU.

    D. Set the priority of the application to Low.

Answer: _____

Question 28

All client computers on your company network run Windows 7 and are members of an Active Directory Domain Services domain. The shipping employees run an application that generates large reports. These reports take too long to generate on the computers. You want to confirm that processor time and memory are acceptable and identify why these reports are generating slowly. If you create a User Defined Data Collector Set which of the following variable information should you collect?

    A. Process\% Privileged Time and Process\% User Time counters for each processor core

    B. Physical Disk\ Avg. Disk Queue Length and Physical Disk\% Disk Time counters for Disk0 of the Computers

    C. Logical Disk\Free Megabytes and Logical Disk\% Free Space counters for the user data drives of the computers

    D. Memory\Available Mbytes and Memory\% Committed Bytes In Use counters

Answer: _____

Question 29

In Windows 7 you can control when users such as kids can login to Windows 7. Which of the following best describes where to configure this option?

    A. You cannot choose this feature unless you are connected to a domain.

    B. Go to the Start, Control Panel, User Accounts and Family Safety, Setup Parental Controls, and then choose Time Restrictions.

    C.   Go to Start, Control Panel. User Profiles, and then Time Restriction Settings.

    D. Go to the Homegroup settings and choose Offline Time Settings.

Answer: _____

Question 30

All client computers on your company network run Windows 7 and are members of an Active Directory Domain Services domain. Each computer has four 1-GB RAM modules and a single physical disk.

When the employees run a three-dimensional (3-D) design application that extensively uses the RAM, they experience slow performance on their computers. You discover that the swap files on the computers are extensively used. What should you do to fix the issue?

    A. Disable the hardware acceleration on the monitor card.

    B. Increase the RAM to 8 GB.

    C. Add a second disk to decrease paging

    D. Configure the virtual memory on the computers so that the initial size of the virtual memory is equal to the maximum size of the virtual memory.

Answer: _____

Question 31

All client computers on your company network run Windows 7 and are members of an Active Directory Domain Services domain. All servers in the network are running Windows Server 2008 R2. The Active Directory Domain Services domain name is mediaworkspublishing.com. Employees access the company intranet using the URL of http:// sharing mediaworkspublishing.com.

Which of the following will allow a single user to access the URL of http://sharing.mediaworkspublishing.com and allow them to see a different server so he can access a new version of the site without affecting other employees' access to the current site??

      A. Add an entry to the Hosts file that specifies sharing.mediaworkspublishing.com and the IP address of the new server on the employee's computer.

      B. Create a sub DNS domain and record for sharing.mediaworksublishing.com that specifies the IP address of the test server.

      C. Use Group Policy to restrict the user from the original server and then use the ROUTEPRINT command to map the new IP address for the server.

      D. All of the above will work.

Answer: _____

Question 32

All client computers on your company network run Windows 7 and are members of an Active Directory Domain Services domain. You deploy network printers. You need to ensure that employees are able to find these printers. What should you do first?

      A. Check to make sure that your print servers include 64-bit Windows 7 print drivers.

      B. Enter the printers IP in the Location Aware Printing utility.

      C. Create a group policy to enable the "Automatically publish new printers."

      D. Do nothing. Printer will automatically appear on all PC's that join the domain as long as they are installed on the domain controller.

Answer: _____

Question 33

To establish a DirectAccess connection to the network, what is the first requirement?

A. Install a certificate

B. Create a VPN connection

C. A static IPv4 address

D. A static IPv6 address

Answer: _____

Question 34

You are the network administrator of a network that has client computers that run Windows 7 and other client computers that run Windows XP Professional. After enabling the Network Discovery feature on the Windows 7 computers you find that the Windows XP computers do not appear on the created network map. What should you do to make them appear on the map?

A. Place the XP computer names in the Computers folder in 'Active Directory.

B. Install the Link Layer Topology Discovery (LLTD) Responder on the Windows XP computers.

C. Add the XP computer names Network Discovery search feature.

C. Map at least one share from the domain controllers on each XP computer.

Answer: _____

Question 35

All client computers on your company network run Windows 7 and are members of an Active Directory Domain Services domain using Windows 2008 R2 servers. Another network administrator changes the IP address of an application server and employees are unable to connect to the server after the change. You need to ensure that the employees are able to connect to the server immediately. Which of the following is the correct fix for the problem?

    A. Use the "net send *" command to send a message to all users instructing them to open the server from its IP address.

    B. Email each user a new Hosts file.

    C. Run a remote Windows PowerShell script to flush the DNS resolver cache on each computer.

    D. Email each user instructions to use

Answer: _____

Question 36

To audit the usage of other users on a shared folder on your Windows 7 computer, which of the following actions should be taken?

    A. Configure the Audit object access setting in the local Group Policy.

    B. Right click on the folder being shared and choose the Audit directory service Access setting.

    C. In the Event Viewer, right click on the System Log. Choose Properties and select all the options for logging including folder access.

    D. Modify the properties of the Security log from the Event Viewer.

Answer: _____

Question 37

You are in charge of a computer that runs Windows 7. You find that an application named Google Desktop runs during the startup process. You have to prevent only Google Desktop from running during the startup process. Users must be allowed to run Google Desktop manually however. What is the proper way to configure this without using third party tools?

A. The msconfig.exe tool should be modified.

B. The application control policy should be modified from the local Group Policy.

C. The software boot policy should be modified from the local Group Policy.

D. The Startup applications in the System Configuration tool should be modified.

Answer: _____

Question 38

You have a Virtual Hard Disk (VHD) with Windows 7 installed and a computer running Windows 7 Ultimate. Which procedure of the following would allow you to book the Windows 7 PC from the VHD?

A. Run bcdedit.exe and modify the Windows Boot Manager.

B. Select vdisk should be run from Diskpart.exe.

C. Modify the BIOS to boot from an ISO.

D. Press F12 at startup and wait for the option to press any key to start from a VHD.

Answer: _____

Question 39

Which of the following is used to control when the security pop-up notifications are used?

        A. Security Control Manager

        B. User Account Control

        C. User Access Control Panel

        D. Notification Control Settings Manager

Answer: _____

Question 32

Which of the following is not a Windows PE tool?

        A. Diskpart

        B. Drvload

        C. Oscdimg

        D. Winpeshl

        E. None of the above.

Answer: _____

Question 40

All 260 client computers on your company network run Windows 7 and are members of an Active Directory Domain Services domain. Your team consists of 20 desktop support technicians who are sent to resolve a hardware issue with a user's computer. Both technicians troubleshoot but get different results by using their own User Defined Data Collector Sets. In order to standardize the Data Collector Set on a network share that is accessible to your team which of the following should you perform?

   A. Create an Event Trace Data Collector Set

   B. Create a Performance Counter Data Collector Set

   C. Create a Performance Counter Alert Data Collector Set Template

   D. Create a System Configuration Information Data Collector Set Template

Answer: _____

Question 41

Which of the following can be used to increase the physical memory on your Windows 7 PC and increase the speed?

   A. PhysiRAM

   B. Aero Glass

   C. DirectAccess

   D: ReadyBoost

Answer: _____

Question 42

A USB external drive is attached to a Windows 7 Professional computer. You want to enable BitLocker To Go on the USB disk. Which of the following must be done?

A. In order to make sure of this, obtain a client certificate from an enterprise certification authority (CA).

B. You must install the Encrypting File System (EFS) from the Add/Remove Windows Components.

C. In order to make sure of this, the computer should be upgraded to Windows 7 Ultimate or Windows 7 Enterprise.

D. You need to download BitLocker To Go from Microsoft's website.

Answer: _____

Question: 43

All client computers on your company network run Windows 7 and are members of an Active Directory Domain Services domain. All servers in the network are running Windows Server 2008 R2. The shipping department staff are all currently local administrators on their computers and are members of the Shipping Global Security Group. A new version of the shipping software application is available on the network.

As the network administrator you are tasked to apply an AppLocker security policy to the Shipping Global Security Group. You need to ensure that members of the Shipping Group are not allowed to upgrade the software on their computers by doing which of the following?

A. Create an Enforce rule restriction based on the version of the software.

B. Move the users to the No Software Install Rights Active Directory Group.

C. Create a certificate with only Enterprise Administrator rights.

D. Create an Enforce rule restriction based on the publisher of the software.

Answer: _____

Question 44

All client computers on your company network run Windows 7 and are members of an Active Directory Domain Services domain. The application control method was established by using Software Restriction Policies. These Software Restriction Policies were deployed in a single Group Policy object (GPO) linked to the Organizational Unit (OU) that contains the computers.

You plan to deploy Microsoft Office 2007 Professional and configure AppLocker for control within the GPO. To ensure that core business applications continue to function, which of the following should be done?

A. Create AppLocker rules and apply them to the Certificate Policy.

B. Move the AppLocker rules to a different GPO.

C. Create a new GPO. Apply the Software Restriction Policy and the AppLocker rules to the new GPO.

D. Create a new AppLocker rules allowing for only digitally signed certificates.

Answer: _____

Question 45

All client computers on your company network run Windows 7. A standard Windows 7 image is loaded on all new computers on the network. Some of the users are complaining that the pen interface is not working on their new tablet PC's. Which of the following will most likely resolve the user's issues?

A. Turn on the Media Features.

B. Turn on the Tablet PC Components.

C. Turn off the keyboard and start the pen service.

D. Turn on OCR Mode.

Answer: _____

Question: 46

All client computers on your company network run Windows 7 and are members of an Active Directory Domain Services domain. All client computers on your company network were recently migrated from Windows XP to Windows 7. The company however uses a custom designed application that is currently not compatible with Windows 7. A shim has been created and applied to eliminate compatibility issues until the software can be made compatible with Windows 7. The developers have given you a security update for the custom application. However, during testing you are unable to install the application. You as the network administrator need to ensure that the application can be installed in the test environment before it can be deployed to the production environment. Which of the following should be performed?

    A. Modify the shim to apply to all versions of the application.

    B. Place and exception so there are no UAC prompts.

    C. Run the .msi file from an elevated command prompt.

    D. Modify the shim to apply only to the new version of the application.

Answer: _____

Question 47

What action would you perform to prevent Internet Explorer from saving any data during a browsing session?

    A. The security settings for the Internet zone should be disabled.

    B. The BranchCache service should be disabled.

    C. The InPrivate Blocking list should be disabled.

    D. Open an InPrivate Browsing session in IE.

Answer: _____

Question 48

All client computers on your company network run Windows 7 and are members of an Active Directory Domain. AppLocker is configured to allow only approved applications to run. Employees with Standard user account permissions are able to run applications that install into the user profile folder. What should you do as the administrator to stop unauthorized applications from being installed?

A. Create Executable Rules by selecting the Create Default Rules option.

B. Create Windows Installer Rules by selecting in Group Policy

C. Create the following Windows Installer Rule: Deny – Everyone - %OSDRIVE%\Users\<user name>\Downloads* -No

D. Go to each PC and remove the local administrator account from the local PC's Administrator Group.

Answer: _____

Question 49

You are in charge of two computers that running Windows 7 called Computer1 and Computer 2. What action should you perform to make sure you can remotely execute commands on Computer02 from Computer01?

A. You should enable Windows Remote Management (WinRM) in the Control Panel on both computers.

B. winrm quickconfig should be run on C01.

C. You should enable Windows Remote Management (WinRM) from the Windows 2008 R2 server in the network

D. winrm quickconfig should be run on C02.

Answer: _____

Question 50

All client computers on your company network run Windows 7. Several legacy software applications are made available on the computers by using Windows XP Mode (XPM). Employees report that all Start menu shortcuts for the legacy applications are missing from their computers. Which of the following is the correct way to allow all the legacy shortcuts to be accessible from the Start menu?

A. Enable the Auto Publish option for Virtual Machine Settings on the Windows 7 computers.

B. Copy the program shortcuts to the Start menu of the Windows 7 computers.

C. Reinstall the applications on the XPM machines on all the Windows 7 computers.

D. All of the above will work.

Answer: _____

Question 51

All client computers on your company network run Windows 7.

An application has stopped working. The application is dependent on a service that runs automatically and logs on to the domain by using a dedicated service account. You also discover that an entry in the event log has the following message: "Logon failure: unknown user name or bad password." You need to ensure that the service runs successfully. What should you do?

A. Add the dedicated account to the local Administrators group.

B. Add the employee user account to the local Administrators group.

C. Reset the employee password and configure it to never expire.

D. Reset the service account password and configure it to never expire.

Answer: D

Answer: _____

Question: 52

You manage a computer that runs Windows 7. Good thing you imaged your PC after you installed Windows 7, because a virus has infected your PC. Which of the following procedures will allow you to restore your PC?

A. Restart computer should be started from Windows Preinstallation Environment (Windows PE) and then ImageLoader.exe should be run.

B. Use the Last Known Good Configuration feature to start the computer.

C. Boot the computer from the Windows 7 DVD and then the Startup Repair tools. Choose system repair using an image.

D. Boot the computer from the Windows 7 DVD and then choose the System Image Recovery tool.

Answer: _____

Question 53

All client computers on your company network run Windows 7 and are members of an Active Directory Domain. All servers in the network are running Windows 2003. After a user attempts to log on to the domain from his computer, he receives the following error message:

> *"System cannot log you on to the domain because the system's computer account in its primary domain is missing or the password on that account is incorrect."*

Which of the following is the correct way to resolve the issue?

A. Change the user's password.

B. Reset the users GUID on the domain controller.

C. Add the user account of the employee to the Enterprise Administrators group.

D. Remove the computer from the domain, place it in a workgroup and then re-add the computer again to the domain.

Answer: _____

Question 54

All client computers on your company network run Windows 7 and are members of an Active Directory Domain Services domain. All servers in the network are running Windows Server 2008 R2. You suspect that a device listed under Non-Plug and Play Drivers in the Device Manager is causing problems. How do you immediately stop the device to determine if the device is the cause?

A. Open the device Properties dialog box in Device Manager. On the Driver tab, change the USB Start Type to Disabled.

B. Open the device Properties dialog box in Device Manager. On the Driver tab, click Stop.

C. Open the device Properties dialog box in Device Manager. On the USB Driver tab, click Disable.

D. Open the device Properties dialog box in Device Manager. On the Driver tab, click Uninstall.

Answer: _____

Question 55

There are multiple users that log on to a Windows 7 Professional computer. You need to deny one user access to removable devices on the computer. All other users must have access to the removable drives. What action should you perform?

A. The settings of all removable devices should be modified from Device Manager.

B. An application control policy should be modified from the local Group Policy.

C. A removable storage access policy should be modified from the local Group Policy.

D. The BitLocker Drive Encryption settings should be modified from Control Panel.

Answer: _____

Question 56

You use a computer that runs Windows 7 Ultimate. You are asked to prevent users from copying unencrypted files to removable drives. What action should you perform?

A. The Trusted Platform System (TPS) settings should be modified from a local Group Policy.

B. TPS should be initialized from the Trusted Platform Settings (TPM) snap-in.

C. The BitLocker Drive Encryption settings should be modified from Control Panel.

D. The BitLocker Drive Encryption settings should be modified from a local Group Policy.

Answer: _____

Question 57

There is a head office and a branch office in your company network. The branch office has computers that run Windows 7 Professional. A network administrator enables BranchCache in the head office. You have to make sure that other computers in the branch office can access the cached content on your computer. So what action should be performed?

A. The Windows Firewall, Advanced Security rules should be modified.

B. Turn on Internet Information Services (IIS).

C. The computer should be configured as a hosted cache client.

D. The BranchCache service should be configured to start automatically on a Windows 2003 server.

Answer: _____

Question 58

All client computers on your company network run Windows 7 and are members of an Active Directory Domain Services domain. The event logs contain errors from an application source as well as the Kernel-Power source. You plan to track these errors to help troubleshoot the problem. To capture only the relevant data to generate a report which of the following should you do?

A. Open Event Viewer and sort by "Source = CRITICAL" only.

B. Open Event Viewer and create a Custom View. Include the application and system logs and include the event sources. Save the filter results as an XML file.

C. Open Event Viewer, go to Properties and create a filter.

D. Use Performance Monitor to create a template EventLog-Application Event Session.

Answer: _____

Question 59

All client computers on your company network run Windows 7 and are members of an Active Directory Domain Services domain. An employee installs several new applications on a computer but notices the computer takes much longer to startup after he logs in. What tool can be used to reduce the startup time?

A. Run the Sysedit command.

B. Use the Startup console to eliminate startup items.

C. Use the Task Manager tool to stop the services.

D. Run the msconfig tool.

Answer: _____

Questions 60

Which of the following permissions are automatically set on a file when you apply the Read & Execute (Deny) NTFS permission? (Choose 2)

      A. List Folder Contents (Deny)

      B. Modify (Deny)

      C. Write (Deny)

      D. Read (Deny)

Answer: _____

Appendix A – Windows PreInstallation Environment (Windows PE)

Windows PreInstallation Environment (Windows PE) 3.0 is a minimal Win32 operating system with limited services, built on the Windows 7 kernel. It is used to prepare a computer for Windows installation, to copy disk images from a network file server, and to initiate Windows Setup.

Windows PE is not designed to be the primary operating system on a computer, but is instead used as a standalone preinstallation environment and as an integral component of other Setup and recovery technologies, such as Setup for Windows 7, Windows Deployment Services (Windows DS), the Systems Management Server (SMS) Operating System (OS) Deployment Feature Pack, and the Windows Recovery Environment (Windows RE).

Windows PE is such a new product and could be a book on its own. Most of the information in these next two sections is taken directly from TechNet.Microsoft.com publically available documentation. We would like to thank Microsoft them for their valuable input.

Benefits of Windows PE

Windows PE was created to help OEMs and IT professionals boot a computer with no functioning operating system.

In the past, OEMs and IT professionals often used an MS-DOS-based boot floppy disk to start a computer. However, an MS-DOS-based boot floppy disk has a number of limitations that make it difficult to use for pre-installing Windows or recovering existing installations or data. It has:

- No support for the NTFS file system.

- No native networking support.

- No support for 32-bit (or 64-bit) Windows device drivers, making it necessary to locate 16-bit drivers.

- Limited support for custom applications and scripts.

- The limitations of MS-DOS-based startup disks led Microsoft to develop Windows PE, which is now the primary Microsoft tool for booting computers with no functioning operating system. Once you boot a computer into Windows PE, you can prepare it for Windows installation, and then initiate Windows Setup from a network or local source. You can also service an existing copy of Windows or recover data.

- Because Windows PE is based on the kernel for Windows 7, it overcomes the limitations of MS-DOS-based boot disks by providing the following capabilities:

- Native support for the NTFS 5.x file system, including dynamic volume creation and management.

- Native support for TCP/IP networking and file sharing (client only).

- Native support for 32-bit (or 64-bit) Windows device drivers.

- Native support for a subset of the Win32 Application Programming Interface (API).

- Optional support for Windows Management Instrumentation (WMI), Microsoft Data Access Component (MDAC) and HTML Application (HTA).

- Ability to start from a number of media types, including CD, DVD, USB flash drive (UFD), and a Remote Installation Services (RIS) server.

- Windows PE offline sessions are supported.

- Windows PE images can be serviced offline.

- Windows PE includes all Hyper-V™ drivers except display drivers. This enables Windows PE to run in Hypervisor. Supported features include mass storage, mouse integration, and network adapters.

Common Windows PE Scenarios

Windows PE is a modified version of the Windows operating system that is designed to support installing Windows and troubleshooting and recovering an installation that can no longer boot.

Windows PE runs every time you install Windows 7. The graphical tools that collect configuration information during the Setup phase are running within Windows PE. In addition, information technology (IT) departments can customize and extend Windows PE to meet their unique deployment needs. Windows PE also provides support for servicing Windows images.

Windows PE Troubleshooting

Windows PE is useful for both automatic and manual troubleshooting. For example, if Windows 7 fails to start because of a corrupted system file, Windows PE can automatically start and launch the Windows Recovery Environment (Windows RE). You can also manually start Windows PE to use built-in or customized troubleshooting and diagnostic tools.

OEMs and independent software vendors (ISVs) can use Windows PE to build customized, automated solutions for recovering and rebuilding computers running Windows 7. For example, users can start their computers from Windows PE recovery CDs or recovery partitions to automatically reformat their hard disks and to reinstall Windows 7 with the original drivers, settings, and applications.

In the next section let's take a look at the Windows PE tools.

Windows PE Tools

Let's take a look at the tools that come with Windows PE as follows:

- BCDboot
- BCDEdit
- Bootsect
- Deployment Image Servicing and Management
- Diskpart
- Drvload
- Oscdimg
- Winpeshl
- Wpeinit
- Wpeutil

BCDBOOT

BCDboot is a tool used to quickly set up a system partition, or to repair the boot environment located on the system partition. The system partition is set up by copying a small set of boot environment files from an installed Windows® image. BCDboot also creates a Boot Configuration Data (BCD) store on the system partition with a new boot entry that enables you to boot to the installed Windows image.

You can run BCDboot from Windows® PE. For information on Windows PE, see Windows PE Walkthroughs.

BCDboot is included with Windows® 7 and Windows Server® 2008 R2 in the %WINDIR%\System32 folder. BCDboot is also available in the Windows OEM Preinstallation Kit (OPK) and Windows Automated Installation Kit (AIK) under the %Program Files%\<version>\Tools directory, where <version> is either Windows OPK or Windows AIK.

BCDboot copies a set of boot environment files from a Windows image that is already on the computer. BCDboot can copy boot environment files from images of Windows Vista®, Windows Server® 2008, Windows 7, or Windows Server 2008 R2. For information on applying a Windows image to a system, see Capture and Apply Windows Images.

BCDboot uses the file: %WINDIR%\System32\Config\BCD-Template file to create a new BCD store and initialize the BCD boot-environment files on the system partition. Specific BCD settings can be defined in the BCD-Template file. The tool also copies the most recent versions of boot-environment files from the operating system image %WINDIR%\boot folder and %WINDIR%\System32 folder to the system partition.

BCDboot copies files to the default system partition identified by the firmware. You can create this partition by using a partitioning tool such as DiskPart. You do not have to assign a drive letter to this partition for BCDboot to locate it. For more information, see the DiskPart Help from the command line, or Diskpart Command line syntax.

On BIOS-based systems, the system partition is the active partition on disks using the Master Boot Record (MBR) disk format. BCDboot creates the \Boot directory on the system partition and copies all required boot-environment files to this directory.

On Unified Extensible Firmware Interface (UEFI)-based systems, the EFI system partition is the system partition on disks using the GUID Partition Table (GPT) disk format. BCDboot creates the \Efi\Microsoft\Boot directory and copies all required boot-environment files to this directory.

BCDboot can update an existing boot environment to the system partition. Newer file versions from the Windows image will be copied to the system partition.

If a BCD store already exists on the system partition:

> BCDboot will create a new boot entry in the existing BCD store, based on settings in the BCD-Template file, and remove any duplicate boot entries that reference the same Windows image.

> If there is already a boot entry for the Windows image, and additional BCD settings are enabled for that boot entry beyond the default values, these settings can be retained the next time BCDboot is run by using the /m option to merge the existing boot entry, identified by the OS Loader GUID into the new boot entry created by BCDboot.

BCEDIT

Boot Configuration Data (BCD) files provide a store that is used to describe boot applications and boot application settings. The objects and elements in the store effectively replace Boot.ini.

BCDEdit is a command-line tool for managing BCD stores. It can be used for a variety of purposes, including creating new stores, modifying existing stores, adding boot menu parameters, and so on. BCDEdit serves essentially the same purpose as Bootcfg.exe on earlier versions of Windows, but with two major improvements:

- Exposes a wider range of boot parameters than Bootcfg.exe.

- Has improved scripting support.

BCDEdit is the primary tool for editing the boot configuration of Windows Vista and later versions of Windows. It is included with the Windows Vista distribution in the %WINDIR%\System32 folder.

BCDEdit is limited to the standard data types and is designed primarily to perform single common changes to BCD. For more complex operations or nonstandard data types, consider using the BCD Windows Management Instrumentation (WMI) application programming interface (API) to create more powerful and flexible custom tools.

Syntaxes

BCDEdit /Command [<Argument1>] [<Argument2>] ...

Parameters

General BCDEdit Command-Line Option

Syntax	Description
/?	Displays a list of BCDEdit commands. Running this command without an argument displays a summary of the available commands. To display detailed help for a particular command, run **bcdedit /?** <command>, where <command> is the name of the command you are searching for more information about. For example, **bcdedit /? createstore** displays detailed help for the Createstore command.

Parameters that Operate on a Store

Syntax	Description
/createstore	Creates a new empty boot configuration data store. The created store is not a system store.
/export	Exports the contents of the system store into a file. This file can be used later to restore the state of the system store. This command is valid only for the system store.
/import	Restores the state of the system store by using a backup data file previously generated by using the **/export** option. This command deletes any existing entries in the system store before the import takes place. This command is valid only for the system store.
/store	This option can be used with most BCDedit commands to specify the store to be used. If this option is not specified, then BCDEdit operates on the system store. Running the **bcdedit /store** command by itself is equivalent to running the **bcdedit /enum active** command.

Parameters that Operate on Entries in a Store

Syntax	Description
/copy	Makes a copy of a specified boot entry in the same system store.

/create	Creates a new entry in the boot configuration data store. If a well-known identifier is specified, then the **/application**, **/inherit**, and **/device** parameters cannot be specified. If an identifier is not specified or not well known, an **/application**, **/inherit**, or **/device** option must be specified.
/delete	Deletes an element from a specified entry.

Parameters that Operate on Entry Options

Syntax	Description
/deletevalue	Deletes a specified element from a boot entry.
/set	Sets an entry option value.

Parameters that Control Output

Syntax	Description
/enum	Lists entries in a store. The **/enum** option is the default value for BCEdit, so running the **bcdedit** command without parameters is equivalent to running the **bcdedit /enum active** command.
/v	Verbose mode. Usually, any well-known entry identifiers are represented by their friendly shorthand form. Specifying **/v** as a command-line option displays all identifiers in full. Running the **bcdedit /v** command by itself is equivalent to running the **bcdedit /enum active /v** command.

Parameters that Control the Boot Manager

Syntax	Description
/bootsequence	Specifies a one-time display order to be used for the next boot. This command is similar to the **/displayorder** option, except that it is used only the next time the computer starts. Afterwards, the computer reverts to the original display order.
/default	Specifies the default entry that the boot manager selects when the timeout expires.
/displayorder	Specifies the display order that the boot manager uses when displaying boot parameters to a user.
/timeout	Specifies the time to wait, in seconds, before the boot manager selects the default entry.
/toolsdisplayorder	Specifies the display order for the boot manager to use when displaying the **Tools** menu.

Parameters that Control Emergency Management Services

Syntax	Description
/bootems	Enables or disables Emergency Management Services (EMS) for the specified entry.
/ems	Enables or disables EMS for the specified operating system boot entry.

/emssettings	Sets the global EMS settings for the computer. **/emssettings** does not enable or disable EMS for any particular boot entry.

Parameters that Control Debugging

Syntax	Description
/bootdebug	Enables or disables the boot debugger for a specified boot entry. Although this command works for any boot entry, it is effective only for boot applications.
/dbgsettings	Specifies or displays the global debugger settings for the system. This command does not enable or disable the kernel debugger; use the **/debug** option for that purpose. To set an individual global debugger setting, use the **bcdedit /set** <dbgsettings> <type> <value> command.
/debug	Enables or disables the kernel debugger for a specified boot entry.

BCDboot Command-line Options

The following command-line options are available for BCDboot.exe.

BCDBOOT source [/llocale] [/svolume-letter] [/v] [/m [{OS Loader GUID}]]

BOOTSECT

Bootsect.exe updates the master boot code for hard disk partitions to switch between Bootmgr and NT Loader (NTLDR). You can use this tool to restore the boot sector on your computer. This tool replaces FixFAT and FixNTFS.

Bootsect Commands

Bootsect uses the following command-line options:

bootsect.exe {/help | /nt52 | /nt60} {**SYS** | **ALL** | <DriveLetter:>} [**/force**] /mbr

For example, to apply the master boot code that is compatible with NTLDR to the volume labeled E, use the following command:

bootsect.exe /nt52 E:

Syntax	Description
/help	Displays these usage instructions.
/nt52	Applies the master boot code that is compatible with NTLDR to **SYS, ALL**, or <DriveLetter>. The operating system installed on **SYS, ALL**, or <DriveLetter> must be Windows® XP.
/nt60	Applies the master boot code that is compatible with Bootmgr to **SYS, ALL**, or <DriveLetter>. The operating system installed on **SYS, ALL**, or <DriveLetter> must be Windows Vista®.

SYS	Updates the master boot code on the system partition used to boot Windows.
ALL	Updates the master boot code on all partitions. The **ALL** option does not necessarily update the boot code for each volume. Instead, this option updates the boot code on volumes that can be used as Windows boot volumes, which excludes any dynamic volumes that are not connected with an underlying disk partition. This restriction is present because boot code must be located at the beginning of a disk partition.
<DriveLetter>	Updates the master boot code on the volume associated with this drive letter. Boot code will not be updated if either: • <DriveLetter> is not associated with a volume • <DriveLetter> is associated with a volume not connected to an underlying disk partition.
/force	Forcibly dismounts the volumes during the boot code update. You must use this option with caution. If Bootsect.exe cannot gain exclusive volume access, then the file system may overwrite the boot code before the next reboot. Bootsect.exe always attempts to lock and dismount the volume before each update. When **/force** is specified, a forced dismount is attempted if the initial lock attempt fails. A lock can fail, for example, if files on the destination volume are currently opened by other programs. When successful, a forced dismount enables exclusive volume access and a reliable boot code update even though the initial lock failed. At the same time, a forced dismount invalidates all open handles to files on the destination volume. This can result in unexpected behavior from the programs that opened these files. Therefore, use this option with caution.
/mbr	Updates the master boot record without changing the partition table on sector 0 of the disk that contains the partition specified by **SYS**, **ALL**, or <drive letter>. When used with the **/nt52** option, the master boot record is compatible with operating systems older than Windows Vista. When used with the **/nt60** option, the master boot record is compatible with Windows® 7, or Windows Server® 2008. For example, to apply the master boot code that is compatible with NTLDR to the volume labeled E:, use the following command: bootsect /nt52 E

Deployment Image Servicing and Management

Deployment Image Servicing and Management (DISM) is a command-line tool used to service Windows® images offline before deployment. You can use it to install, uninstall, configure, and update Windows features, packages, drivers, and international settings. Subsets of the DISM servicing commands are also available for servicing a running operating system.

DISM is installed with Windows 7, and it is also distributed in the Windows OEM Preinstallation Kit (Windows OPK) and the Windows Automated Installation Kit (Windows AIK). It can be used to service Windows Vista with Service Pack 1 (SP1), Windows Server 2008, Windows 7, Windows Server 2008 R2, or Windows PE images. DISM replaces several Windows OPK tools, including PEimg, Intlcfg, and Package Manager.

DISM Command-Line Options

To service an offline Windows image, you must first mount the image. You can use Windows image (WIM) commands and arguments to mount a WIM image for servicing and management. You can also use these commands to list the indexes or verify the architecture for the image you are mounting. After you update the image, you must unmount it and either commit or discard the changes you have made.

The following commands can be used to mount, unmount, and query WIM files. These options are not case sensitive.

Syntax	Argument
/Mount-Wim	/WimFile:<*path_to_image.wim*> /Index:<*image_index*>
	/Name:<*image_name*>
	/MountDir:
	<*path_to_mount_directory*>
	/ReadOnly
/Commit-Wim	/MountDir:
	<*path_to_mount_directory*>

The base syntax for nearly all DISM commands is the same. After you have mounted or applied your Windows image so that it is available offline as a flat file structure, you can specify any DISM options, the servicing command that will update your image, and the location of the offline image. You can use only one servicing command per command line. If you are servicing a running computer, you can use the **/Online** option instead of specifying the location of the offline Windows Image.

The base syntax for DISM is:

DISM.exe {**/Image:**<*path_to_image*> | **/Online**} [dism_options] {servicing_command} [<*servicing_argument*>]

The following DISM options are available for an offline image.

DISM.exe /image:<*path_to_offline_image_directory*> [**/WinDir:**<*path_to_%WINDIR%*>] [**/LogPath:**<*path_to_log_file.log*>] [**/LogLevel:**<n>] [**SysDriveDir:**<*path_to_bootMgr_file*>] [**/Quiet**] [**/NoRestart**] [**/ScratchDir:**<*path_to_scratch_directory*>]

The following DISM options are available for a running operating system.

DISM.exe /online [**/LogPath:**<*path_to_log_file*>] [**/LogLevel:**<*n*>] [**/Quiet**]
[**/NoRestart**] [**/ScratchDir:**<*path_to_scratch_directory*>]

DISKPART

DiskPart is a text-mode command interpreter that enables you to manage objects (disks, partitions, or volumes) by using scripts or direct input from a command prompt. Before you can use DiskPart commands, you must first list, and then select an object to give it focus. When an object has focus, any DiskPart commands that you type will act on that object.

You can list the available objects and determine an object's number or drive letter by using the list disk, list volume, and list partition commands. The list disk and list volume commands display all disks and volumes on the computer. However, the list partition command only displays partitions on the disk that has focus. When you use the list commands, an asterisk (*) appears next to the object with focus. You select an object by its number or drive letter, such as disk 0, partition 1, volume 3, or volume C.

When you select an object, the focus remains on that object until you select a different object. For example, if the focus is set on disk 0 and you select volume 8 on disk 2, the focus shifts from disk 0 to disk 2, volume 8. Some commands automatically change the focus. For example, when you create a new partition, the focus automatically switches to the new partition.

You can only give focus to a partition on the selected disk. When a partition has focus, the related volume (if any) also has focus. When a volume has focus, the related disk and partition also have focus if the volume maps to a single specific partition. If this is not the case, focus on the disk and partition is lost.

Diskpart / <*Syntax*>

The available syntaxes are:

Active, Add, Assign, Attributes, Automount, Break, Clean, Convert, Create, Delete, Detail, Exit, Extend, Filesystems, Format, GPT, Help, Import, Inactive, List, Offline, Online, Recover, Rem, Remove, Repair, Rescan, Retain, Select, Setid, Shrink, Uniqueid.

> **NOTE:** *There are just too many options and syntaxes for this to place in this book. I recommend that you study the items at this link:*
>
> *http://technet.microsoft.com/en-us/library/cc770877(WS.10).aspx*

DRVLOAD

The Drvload tool adds out-of-box drivers to a booted Windows® PE image. It takes one or more driver .inf files as inputs. To add a driver to an offline Windows PE image, use the Deployment Image Servicing and Management (DISM) tool.

If the driver .inf file requires a reboot, Windows PE will ignore the request. If the driver .sys file requires a reboot, then the driver cannot be added with Drvload.

The following command-line options are available for Drvload.

drvload.exe *inf_path* [*,inf_path* [...]] [/?]

Syntax	Description
/?	Displays usage information.
inf_path	Specifies the path to the driver .inf file. The path can contain environment variables.

OSCDIMG

Oscdimg is a command-line tool for creating an image file (.iso) of a customized 32-bit or 64-bit version of Windows® PE. You can then burn the .iso file to a CD-ROM or DVD-ROM. Oscdimg supports ISO 9660, Joliet, and Universal Disk Format (UDF) file systems.

Oscdimg Command-Line Options

The following command-line options are available for Oscdimg.

oscdimg [*options*] *SourceLocationTargetFile*

Syntax	Description
-a	Displays the allocation summary for files and directories.
-b *location*	Specifies the location of the El Torito boot sector file. Do not use any spaces, for example, **-bC:\Directory\Etfsboot.com**
-c	Specifies to use ANSI file names instead of OEM file names.
-d	Does not force lowercase file names to uppercase.
-e	This option disables floppy disk emulation in the El Torito catalog. This option can only be used for single boot entry images and can not be combined with any multi-boot entry switches.
-g	Uses the Universal Coordinated Time (UCT) for all files rather than the local time.

-h	Includes hidden files and directories.
-j1	Encodes Joliet Unicode file names and generates DOS-compatible 8.3 file names in the ISO 9660 namespace. These file names can be read by either Joliet systems or conventional ISO 9660 systems, but Oscdimg may change some of the file names in the ISO 9660 name space to comply with DOS 8.3 and/or ISO 9660 naming restrictions. When using the **-j1**, **-j2**, or **-js** options, the **-d**, **-n**, and **-nt** options do not apply and cannot be used.
-j2	Encodes Joliet Unicode file names without standard ISO 9660 names. (Requires a Joliet operating system to read files from the CD-ROM.) When using the **-j1**, **-j2**, or **-js** options, the **-d**, **-n**, and **-nt** options do not apply and cannot be used.
-js	Overrides the default text file used with the **-j2** option, for example, **-jsc:\Readme.txt** When using the **-j1**, **-j2**, or **-js** options, the **-d**, **-n**, and **-nt** options do not apply and cannot be used.
-k	Creates an image even if it fails to open some of the source files.
-l *labelname*	Specifies the volume label. Do not use spaces between the l and *labelname*. For example, **-lMYLABEL**
-m	Ignores the maximum size limit of an image.
-maxsize: *limit*	Overrides the default maximum size of an image. The default value is a 74-minute CD, unless UDF is used, in which case, the default is that there is no maximum size. The *limit* value is specified in megabytes (MB). For example, **-maxsize:4096** limits the image to 4096 MB. The **-m** option cannot be used with this option.
-n	Enables long file names.
-nt	Enables long file names that are compatible with Windows NT 3.51.
-o	Optimizes storage by encoding duplicate files only once using a MD5 hashing algorithm to compare files.
-oc	Optimizes storage by encoding duplicate files only once using a binary comparison of each file. This option is slower than the **-o** option.
-oi	Optimizes storage by encoding duplicate files only once. When comparing files, ignores Diamond compression timestamps.
-os	Optimizes storage by encoding duplicate files only once. Shows duplicate files when creating the image.
-ois	Optimizes storage by encoding duplicate files only once. When comparing files, ignores Diamond compression timestamps. Shows duplicate files when creating the image.
-p	Specifies the value to use for the Platform ID in the El Torito catalog. The default is 0x00 to represent the x86 platform. This option can only be used for single-boot entry-images and cannot be combined with any multi-boot entry switches.

-q	Scans the source files only; it does not create an image.
-t *mm/dd/yyyy,hh:mm:ss*	Specifies the timestamp for all files and directories. Do not use any spaces. Use the United States of America date format and a 24-hour clock. You can use any delimiter between the items. For example, -t12/31/2000,15:01:00
-u1	Produces an image that has both the UDF file system and the ISO 9660 file system. The ISO 9660 file system will be written with DOS-compatible 8.3 file names. The UDF file system will be written with Unicode file names. This option cannot be combined with the **-n, -nt,** or **-d** options.
-u2	Produces an image that has only the UDF file system on it. Any system not capable of reading UDF will only see a default text file alerting the user that this image is only available on computers that support UDF. This option cannot be combined with the **-n, -nt,** or **-d** options.
-ur	Overrides the default text file used with the **-u2** option. Example: -urc:\Readme.txt This option cannot be combined with the **-n, -nt,** or **-d** options.
-us	Creates sparse file when available. This can only be used with the **-u2** option. This option cannot be combined with the **-n, -nt,** or **-d** options.
-ue	Creates embedded files. This can only be used with the **-u2** option. This option cannot be combined with the **-n, -nt,** or **-d** options.
-uf	Embeds UDF file identifier entries. This can only be used with the **-u2** option. This option cannot be combined with the **-n, -nt,** or **-d** options.
-uv	Specifies UDF Video Zone compatibility during DVD Video/Audio disk creation. This means UDF 1.02 and ISO 9660 are written to the disk. Also, all files in the VIDEO_TS, AUDIO_TS, and JACKET_P directories are written first. These directories take precedence over all other ordering rules used for this image. This option cannot be combined with the **-n, -nt, -d, -j1, -j2, -js, -u1, -u2, -ur, -us, -ue, -uf,** or **-yl** options.
-ut	Truncates the ISO 9660 portion of the image during DVD video/audio disk creation. When this option is used, only the VIDEO_TS, AUDIO_TS, and JACKET_P directories are visible from the ISO 9660 file system. This option cannot be combined with the **-n, -nt, -d, -j1, -j2, -js, -u1, -u2, -ur, -us, -ue, -uf,** or **-yl** options.
-w1	Reports all file names or depths that are not ISO-compliant or Joliet-compliant.
-w2	Reports all file names that are not DOS-compliant.
-w3	Reports all zero-length files.
-w4	Reports each file name that is copied to the image.
-x	Computes and encodes the AutoCRC value in the image.
-yd	Suppresses warnings for non-identical files with the same initial 64,000 bytes.

-yl	Specifies long allocation descriptors instead of short allocation descriptors. This option cannot be combined with the **-n**, **-nt**, or **-d** options.
-y5	Specifies file layout on disk. This option writes all files in an i386 directory first and in reverse sort order.
-y6	Specifies that directory records be exactly aligned at the end of sectors.
-yo	Specifies file layout on disk. This option specifies a text file that has a layout for the files to be placed in the image. The rules for this file are listed below.

    1.   The order file must be in ANSI.

    2.   The order file must end in a new line.

    3.   The order file must have one file per line.

    4.   Each file must be specified relative to the root of the image.

    5.   Each file must be specified as a long file name. No short names are allowed.

    6.   Each file path cannot be longer than MAX_PATH, including volume name.

Note that not all files must be listed in the order file. Any files that are not listed in this file will be ordered as they would be by default in the absence of an ordering file.

-yw	Opens source files with write sharing.
SourceLocation	Required. Specifies the location of the files that you intend to build into an .iso image.
TargetFile	Specifies the name of the .iso image file.

Creating DVD images

For images larger than 4.5 GB, you must create a boot order file (Bootorder.txt) to ensure boot files are located at the beginning of the image. For example,

oscdimg -m -n –yoC:\temp\bootorder.txt -bC:\winpe_x86\etfsboot.com

Where bootorder.txt contains the following list of files.

boot\bcd

boot\boot.sdi

boot\bootfix.bin

boot\bootsect.exe

boot\etfsboot.com

boot\memtest.efi

boot\memtest.exe

boot\en-us\bootsect.exe.mui

boot\fonts\chs_boot.ttf

boot\fonts\cht_boot.ttf

boot\fonts\jpn_boot.ttf

boot\fonts\kor_boot.ttf

boot\fonts\wgl4_boot.ttf

sources\boot.wim

WINPESHI

Winpeshl.ini controls whether a customized shell is loaded in Windows® PE or the default Command Prompt window. To load a customized shell, create a file named Winpeshl.ini and place it in %SYSTEMROOT%\System32 of your customized Windows PE image. The .ini file must have the following sections and entries.

[LaunchApp]

AppPath = %SYSTEMDRIVE%\myshell.exe

[LaunchApps]

%SYSTEMDRIVE%\mydir\application1.exe, {option}

Set the AppPath entry to the path to your shell application. You can use a fully qualified path, or you can use environment variables, such as %SYSTEMROOT%\System32\Myshell.exe. The AppPath entry does not support command-line options.

Use the [LaunchApps] section to run applications with command-line options. The applications run in the order listed. Separate the name of the application from its options with a comma.

When you exit the Command Prompt window or your customized shell application, Windows PE restarts.

> **ALERT:** *Do not edit the value of CmdLine in the HKEY_LOCAL_MACHINE\SYSTEM\Setup registry key of Setupreg.hiv to start your shell application.*

WPEINIT

Wpeinit is a command-line tool that initializes Windows® PE each time that Windows PE boots. When Windows PE boots, Winpeshl.exe executes the Startnet.cmd command script, which launches Wpeinit.exe. Specifically, Wpeinit.exe installs Plug and Play devices, processes Unattend.xml settings, and loads network resources.

Wpeinit replaces the initialization function previously supported in Factory.exe - winpe. Wpeinit outputs log messages to c:\Windows\system32\wpeinit.log.

Wpeinit Command-Line Options

You can manually execute Wpeinit from a Windows PE **Command Prompt** window to process a custom answer file. Wpeinit.exe accepts one option called **-unattend**. You can specify the parameter in one of four ways:

wpeinit -unattend=<path\unattend>

wpeinit -unattend:<path\unattend>

wpeinit /unattend=<path\unattend>

wpeinit /unattend:<path\unattend>

WPEUTIL

The Windows® PE utility (Wpeutil) is a command-line tool that enables you to run various commands in a Windows PE session. For example, you can shut down or restart Windows PE, enable or disable a firewall, set language settings, and initialize a network.

Wpeutil Command-Line Options

Wpeutil uses the following conventions.

wpeutil {command} [*argument*]

For example,

wpeutil shutdown

wpeutil enablefirewall

wpeutil SetMuiLanguage de-DE

Command	Description
CreatePageFile [**/path**=<*path*>] [**/size**=<*size*>]	Creates a page file to a specified path and size. Default path is **C:\pagefile.sys** and size is 64 megabytes. At least one option must be specified. For example, wpeutil CreatePageFile /path=C:\pagefile.sys.
DisableExtendedCharactersForVolume <*path on target volume*>	Disables extended character support for DOS-compatible file names (8.3 format) for the volume containing <*path on target volume*>. <*path on target volume*> must specify the root of the volume, for example C:\. If disabled, all files that have been created with extended characters will be converted to a short filename. This command only applies to NTFS volumes.
DisableFirewall	Disables a firewall. This command does not require any arguments.
EnableExtendedCharactersForVolume <*path on target volume*>	Allows 8.3 format file names to contain extended characters on the volume containing <*path on target volume*>. <*path on target volume*> must specify the root of the volume, for example C:\. This command only applies to NTFS volumes.
EnableFirewall	Enables a firewall. This command does not require any arguments.
InitializeNetwork	Initializes network components and drivers, and sets the computer name to a randomly-chosen value.

ListKeyboardLayouts *<LCID>*	Lists the supported keyboard layouts (Name and ID) for a given Locale ID (LCID) value. The keyboard layouts will also be updated in the registry under the key: **HKLM\SOFTWARE\Microsoft\Windows NT\CurrentVersion\WinPE\KeyboardLayouts**. For a list of valid Locale IDs. For example, wpeutil ListKeyboardLayouts 0x0409 -or- wpeutil ListKeyboardLayouts 1033
Reboot	Restarts the current Windows PE session. 📝Note You can restart the current Windows PE session by running the following wpeutil.exe commands: ▶ **wpeutil shutdown** ▶ **wpeutil reboot**
Saveprofile	Stops logging and saves the custom profile to the location the user specified earlier with the **DISM /enable-profiling** command. For more information on the **/enable-profiling** command-line option. wpeutil Saveprofile < profile_file_name > "short description"
SetKeyboardLayout *<keyboard layout ID>*	Sets the keyboard layout in the current Windows PE session. This will take effect for processes after the command succeeds. To obtain a list of supported keyboard layouts, run ListKeyboardLayouts *<LCID>*. To set the keyboard for en-US, use wpeutil SetKeyboardLayout 0409:00000409
SetMuiLanguage *<language-name>*[;*<language-name>*]	Sets the language. *<language-name>* uses the international language code format (for example, en-US for the U.S. English language). You can specify multiple languages in priority order, by separating them with a semicolon. For example, wpeutil SetMuiLanguage de-DE;en-US
SetUserLocale *<language-name>*[;*<language-name>*]	Sets the user locale. *<language-name>* uses the international language code format (for example, en-US for the U.S. English language). You can specify multiple languages in priority order, by separating them with a semicolon. For example, wpeutil SetUserLocale de-DE;en-US
Shutdown	Shuts down the current Windows PE session.
UpdateBootInfo	Updates information about the method used to boot Windows PE. Information is stored in the registry in the key **HKLM\SYSTEM\CurrentControlSet\Control**. The results of this operation might change after loading additional driver support.
WaitForRemoveableStorage	During the Windows PE startup sequence, this command will block startup until the removable storage devicesare initialized.

Appendix B - Scanstate Migration Tool

The User State Migration Toolkit (USMT) for Windows 7 allows you to determine which migration store type best meets your needs. It allows you to determine how much space is required to run the Microsoft Windows 7 on the source and destination computers. It will also determine the space needed to create and host the migration store, whether you are using a local share, network share, or storage device. It is a very powerful tool.

Let's take a look at the different ways you can run this tool looking at the following:

- Hard-Link Migration Store
- Running ScanState
- Offline Windows Images
- Volume Shadow Copy Support

Hard-Link Migration Store:

Hard-link migration stores are stored locally on a computer that is being reinstalled and can be used to migrate user accounts, files, and settings in less time using megabytes of disk space instead of gigabytes.

Running ScanState

ScanState is a Windows PE command. USMT now supports migration from previous installations of Windows contained in Windows.old directories. This directory is created if you do a full install of Windows 7 and contains all the old Windows installation files including the User folders.

Offline Windows Images

The offline directory can be a Windows directory when you run the ScanState command in Windows PE or the Windows.old when you run the ScanState command in Windows.

Volume Shadow Copy Support

With the /vsc syntax used with the State command allows you to use the volume shadow copy service to capture files that are locked for editing by other applications.

Configurable File Errors

The Config.xml file to configure which file or registry read/write errors can be safely ignored by the /c command-line option and which ones might cause the migration to fail. In addition, the /genconfig option now generates a sample <ErrorControl> section that is enabled by specifying error codes and desired behaviors in the Config.xml file.

> **Sidebar:** New Helper Functions: The ScanState command has two new helper functions called the *Offline Windows Imagescan* or the *MigXmlHelper.GenerateDocPatterns* that enable new migration scenarios:
>
>> **Offline Windows Imagescan** be used to control which files are migrated, based on properties that you specify. For example, date created, date modified, date accessed, and file size.
>>
>> **MigXmlHelper.GenerateDocPatterns** can be used to find user documents on a computer automatically without your having to author extensive custom migration .xml files.
>
> **Note:** *If you add the /listfiles syntax to the Scanstate command you can generate a text file list of all files included in the migration.*

Usmtutils.exe

This is a new tool that supplements the functionality provided by Scanstate.exe and Loadstate.exe.

Local Group Migration

You can use the new <ProfileControl> section in the Config.xml file to configure local group membership of users during the migration. Such as the local administrators group as being members of the local users group during a migration

> ### Sidebar: Plan Your Migration
>
> 1. Depending on whether your migration scenario is refreshing or replacing computers, you can choose an online migration or an offline migration using Windows PE or Windows.old.
>
> 2. Determine What to Migrate such as end-user information, applications settings, operating-system settings, files, folders, and registry keys.
>
> 3. Determine where to store data. Depending on the size of your migration store, you can store the data remotely, locally in a hard-link

migration store or on a local external storage device, or directly on the destination computer.

4. Utilize the /genmigxml syntax to help determine which files will be included in your migration, and to determine if any modifications are necessary.

5. Modify the Migration.xml and MigDocs.xml files, and create custom .xml files, if necessary to identify what to migrate such as the Documents, etc.

6. The document finder MigXmlHelper.GenerateDocPatterns, is a helper function that can be used to automatically find user documents on a computer without authoring extensive custom migration .xml files.

7. Create a Config.xml File if you want to exclude any components from the migration. To create this file, specify the /genconfig option along with the other .xml files when you use the ScanState command.

scanstate /genconfig:config.xml /i:miguser.xml /i:migapp.xml /v:13 /l:scanstate.log

8. Review the migration state of the components listed in the Config.xml file, and specify migrate=no for any that you do not want to migrate.

Using ScanState

1. Back up the source computer.

2. Close all applications.

3. Run the ScanState command on the source computer to collect files and settings. You should specify all of the .xml files that you want the ScanState command to use.

> scanstate \\fileserver\migration\mystore /config:config.xml /i:miguser.xml /i:migapp.xml /v:13 /l:scan.log

4. Prepare the Destination Computer and Restore Files and Settings by installing the operating system on the destination computer.

5. Install all applications that were on the source computer. Although it is not always essential, it is good practice to install all applications on the destination computer before restoring the user state. This ensures that migrated settings are preserved.

> **ALERT:** *The application versions that are installed on the destination computer should be the same version as the one on the source computer.*

6. Close all applications on the Destination Computer

7. Run the LoadState command on the destination computer. Specify the same set of .xml files that you specified when using the ScanState command. However, you do not have to specify the Config.xml file, unless you want to exclude some of the files and settings that you migrated to the store.

For example, the following command migrates the files and settings to a destination computer running Windows Vista or Windows 7:

loadstate \\fileserver\migration\mystore /config:config.xml /i:miguser.xml /i:migapp.xml /v:13 /l:load.log

8 .Log off after you run the LoadState command. Some settings (for example, fonts, wallpaper, and screensaver settings) will not take effect until the next time the user logs on.

Assess Yourself Answers - Are you Ready for the Exam?

1.	D	31.	A
2.	A	32.	C
3.	A	33.	D
4.	C	34.	B
5.	D	35.	C
6.	C	36.	A
7.	A	37.	D
8.	D	38.	A
9.	D	39.	B
10.	C	40.	B
11.	D	41.	D
12.	D	42.	C
13.	B	43.	A
14.	C	44.	B
15.	C	45.	B
16.	D	46.	A
17.	D	47.	D
18.	B, D	48.	A
19.	A, D	49.	D
20.	C	50.	A
21.	C	51.	D
22.	D	52.	D
23.	C	53.	D
24.	C	54.	B
25.	B	55.	C
26.	A	56.	D
27.	D	57.	A
28.	B	58.	B
29.	B	59.	D
30.	D	60.	A,D

Assess Yourself Answers - Are you Ready for the Exam?

1.	D	31.	A
2.	A	32.	C
3.	A	33.	D
4.	C	34.	B
5.	D	35.	C
6.	C	36.	A
7.	A	37.	D
8.	D	38.	A
9.	D	39.	B
10.	C	40.	B
11.	D	41.	D
12.	D	42.	C
13.	B	43.	A
14.	C	44.	B
15.	C	45.	B
16.	D	46.	A
17.	D	47.	D
18.	B, D	48.	A
19.	A, D	49.	D
20.	C	50.	A
21.	C	51.	D
22.	D	52.	D
23.	C	53.	D
24.	C	54.	B
25.	B	55.	C
26.	A	56.	D
27.	D	57.	A
28.	B	58.	B
29.	B	59.	D
30.	D	60.	A,D

INDEX

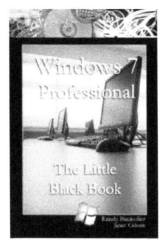

**Windows 7 Professional
The Little Black Book
By: Randy Bankofier**

**SEO For 2010
By: Sean Odom and Sean R. Odom**